Ancient Rome Trivia

Journey into the Rise and Fall of the Republic and Empire with 500 Captivating Questions and Answers

Welcome Aboard, Check Out This Limited-Time Free Bonus!

Ahoy, reader! Welcome to the Ahoy Publications family, and thanks for snagging a copy of this book! Since you've chosen to join us on this journey, we'd like to offer you something special.

Check out the link below for a FREE e-book filled with delightful facts about American History.

But that's not all - you'll also have access to our exclusive email list with even more free e-books and insider knowledge. Well, what are ye waiting for? Click the link below to join and set sail toward exciting adventures in American History.

Access your bonus here

https://ahoypublications.com/

Or, Scan the QR code!

Table of Contents

Introduction

Welcome to the world of ancient Rome. This trivia book will take you on a journey through time, exploring some of this powerful empire's most influential and remarkable aspects, from its foundation to its fall.

We'll uncover stories regarding Roman expansion, wars with Carthage and Greece, religious practices, scientific advancements, literature that shaped our view of today's world, art that still inspires us centuries after it was created, music that continues to be heard around the globe—and much more.

You'll discover incredible facts about all these events and their lasting impact, from Julius Caesar changing history forever to Constantine I leading an unprecedented Christianization effort for his people.

We'll explore political institutions, legal developments, and social class hierarchy while also peeking into day-to-day life in ancient Rome, including agricultural practices and foreign relations.

Finally, we'll finish off by looking at the Latin language and its direct influence on modern languages. This book is an in-depth exploration of ancient Rome, full of surprising facts that will surely captivate any reader's curiosity. So, let's get started.

Foundation of Rome

Discover the incredible story of how Rome came to be. Test your knowledge about the foundation of this legendary city with this collection of ancient Rome trivia questions. How much do you know about the Greek gods and other influential figures who helped shape ancient Roman history? Find out by answering these fascinating questions that cover topics such as when exactly Rome was founded, what two brothers are credited with its traditional founding, how long it took to build walls around the new city-state, and more. So, put on your thinking cap and explore everything there is to know about the amazing beginnings of one of the world's oldest civilizations.

1. When was Rome founded?

    a. 753 BCE

    b. Eighth century CE

    c. 476 CE

    d. 1798 CE

2. The traditional founding of Rome is credited to which two brothers?

    a. Romulus and Remus

    b. Caesar and Augustus

    c. Nero and Caligula

    d. Paulus and Titus

3. Who raised the twins after their parents abandoned them?

    a. A she-wolf

    b. Shepherds from Alba Longa

    c. Greek gods

    d. Julius Caesar

4. What did the twin brothers do when they grew up?

    a. They conquered Greece

    b. They fought with each other for power

    c. They allied with Etruscan cities

    d. All of the above

5. How many hills make up ancient Rome's landscape?

    a. Three

    b. Seven

    c. Twelve

    d. Fourteen

6. What is the name of the hill on which the original city of Rome was founded?

    a. Palatine Hill

    b. Aventine Hill

    c. Capitoline Hill

    d. Quirinal Hill

7. Who were the earliest known inhabitants of Rome?

    a. The Etruscans

    b. The Latins

    c. Greeks

    d. Romans

8. According to Roman mythology, who ordered Remus and Romulus to be thrown into the river Tiber?

    a. Mars

    b. Amulius

    c. Rhea Silvia

    d. None of the above

9. According to Roman mythology, Remus and Romulus were the descendants of which god?

a. Jupiter

b. Mercury

c. Tarquinia

d. Mars

10. How many kings did Rome have?

a. Four

b. Five

c. Six

d. Seven

11. Who was the first king of Rome?

a. Romulus

b. Remus

c. Ancus Marcius

d. Julius Caesar

12. When is the founding of Rome commemorated?

a. May 6

b. April 21

c. June 30

d. None of the above

13. Which god is considered the protector of Rome?

a. Jupiter

b. Mars

c. Apollo

d. Neptune

14. What was the official language spoken in ancient Rome?

a. Latin

b. Greek

c. Italian

d. Sanskrit

15. Who became king after the death of Romulus?

    a. Ancus Marcius

    b. Tarquinius Superbus

    c. Numa Pompilius

    d. None of the above

16. Who wrote the *Aeneid*, an epic poem about the founding of Rome?

    a. Virgil

    b. Ovid

    c. Julius Caesar

    d. Homer

17. Who is Aeneas, the main character of the *Aenid*?

    a. The main rival of Remus and Romulus

    b. The first general of Rome

    c. An ancestor of the Romans

    d. None of the above

18. According to the *Aenid*, Aeneas had participated in which war?

    a. The Trojan War

    b. The Peloponnesian War

    c. The Punic War

    d. None of the above

19. Who wrote the "Twelve Tables," which laid out basic rules for citizens to follow?

    a. Virgil

    b. Julius Caesar

    c. Cicero

    d. No one knows

20. Until when did the monarchy last in Rome?

    a. 600 BCE

    b. 509 BCE

    c. 437 BCE

    d. 101 BCE

ANSWERS

1. a. 753 BCE
2. a. Romulus and Remus
3. a. A she-wolf
4. b. They fought each other for power
5. b. Seven
6. a. Palatine Hill
7. b. The Latins
8. b. Amulius
9. d. Mars
10. d. Seven
11. a. Romulus
12. b. April 21
13. a. Jupiter
14. a. Latin
15. c. Numa Pompilius
16. a. Virgil
17. c. An ancestor of the Romans
18. a. The Trojan War
19. d. No one knows
20. b. 509 BCE

Roman Kingdom and Expansion

This chapter will take a deep dive into the interesting history of the Roman Kingdom and its subsequent expansion. We'll explore some interesting facts about how laws were formed, Roman religion before Christianity, who gained power in Rome during this period, and much more. Get ready to tackle challenging questions that span over two thousand years, from unsolved mysteries like King Tarquin's fate to famous figures like Servius Tullius and Livy, whose works have survived through time. Without further ado, let's begin our journey back in time.

21. What was the name of Rome's first assembly?

    a. Comitia Curiata

    b. Centumviri

    c. Senatus Populusque Romanus (SPQR)

    d. Consilium Plebis

22. How did the Etruscans influence Rome during its early years?

    a. The Romans adopted much of their culture and laws

    b. They provided large sums of money to fund public projects

    c. They built an army for Rome to conquer other territories

    d. All the above

23. Who was the first Etruscan king of Rome?

    a. Lucius Tarquinius Superbus

    b. Lucius Tarquinius Priscus

    c. Ancus Marcius

    d. Servius Tullius

24. What was the main religion of Rome before Christianity?

    a. Paganism

    b. Taoism

    c. Zoroastrianism

    d. Buddhism

25. Where were the Twelve Tables displayed in ancient Rome?

    a. Palace of the king

    b. Rome's Forum

    c. Temple of Jupiter

    d. None of the above

26. Who was the last king of Rome?

    a. Lucius Tarqiunius Superbus

    b. Julius Caesar

    c. Servius Tullius

    d. None of the above

27. How did the Roman Kingdom come to an end in 509 BCE?

    a. It was overthrown

    b. It collapsed because of a natural disaster

    c. It was conquered by the Etruscans

    d. All of the above

28. Who was the first Roman consul appointed in 509 BCE?

    a. Publius Valerius Publicola

    b. Marcus Tullius Cicero

    c. Lucius Junius Brutus

    d. Titus Livy

29. What incident brought about the end of the Roman Kingdom?

    a. Invasion of Gaul

    b. Rape of Lucretia

    c. First Punic War

    d. Freeing of slaves

30. How did the first four kings of Rome ascend the throne after Romulus?

    a. They were proclaimed by the army in coups

    b. They were elected by the Comitia Curiata

    c. They succeeded the throne in hereditary fashion

    d. None of the above

31. In which year were the Twelve Tables formally enacted?

    a. 566 BCE

    b. 449 BCE

    c. 616 BCE

    d. 464 BCE

32. Which Roman god was adopted from the Etruscans?

    a. Jupiter

    b. Apollo

    c. Diana

    d. Mars

33. Who wrote the *History of Rome*, the earliest surviving account of early Rome?

    a. Titus Livius

    b. Augustus

    c. Caesar

    d. Cicero

34. How did Tarquinius Superbus increase his power in Rome?

    a. He limited citizens' rights and strengthened the monarchy

    b. He raised taxes to fund public projects

    c. He formed strong military alliances with other cities

    d. All of the above

35. From which Latin tribe did the Romans adopt many customs and religious beliefs?

    a. Sabines

    b. Calabrians

    c. Gauls

    d. Samnites

36. In 509 BCE, what were the two main classes in Roman society according to wealth?

a. Patricians and plebeians

b. Slaves and free men

c. Peasants and nobles

d. Diviners and rhetoricians

37. Who is said to have created the Roman Senate?

a. Tarquinius Superbus

b. Romulus

c. Lucius Junius Brutus

d. Julius Caesar

38. How did the Senate gain power during the Roman Republic?

a. By taking control over political, military, and religious decisions

b. By forming alliances with other cities

c. By proposing laws to strengthen the monarchy

d. All of the above

39. How many members were originally in the Roman Senate?

a. 500

b. 400

c. 150

d. 100

40. What was the highest elected public official called in the Roman Republic?

a. Dictator

b. Consul

c. King

d. Minister

ANSWERS

21. a. Comitia Curiata
22. a. Romans adopted much of their culture and laws
23. b. Lucius Tarquinius Priscus
24. a. Paganism
25. b. Rome's Forum
26. a. Lucius Tarquinius Superbus
27. a. It was overthrown
28. c. Lucius Junius Brutus
29. b. Rape of Lucretia
30. b. They were elected by the Comitia Curiata
31. c. 449 BCE
32. a. Jupiter
33. a. Titus Livius
34. d. All of the above
35. a. Sabines
36. a. Patricians and plebeians
37. b. Romulus
38. a. By taking control over political, military, and religious decisions
39. d. 100
40. b. Consul

The Punic Wars and the Republic

Have you ever wondered what it was like to live in ancient Rome? What historical occurrences led to its rise to prominence as one of the most potent civilizations in history? In this chapter, we'll examine a fascinating period of Roman history, covering several key aspects contributing to Rome's success. Answer questions on Roman Republic reforms, the reasons for the First Punic War, and other topics to see how much you know. Travel back in time to explore what life was like during these crucial battles that eventually determined Rome's future.

41. Which empire did Rome go to war with during the Punic Wars?

    a. Hyksos

    b. Carthage

    c. Gaul

    d. Persia

42. What was the cause of the First Punic War?

    a. Conflict over Sicily

    b. Conflict between Roman and Etruscan forces

    c. A trade dispute between Carthage and Rome

    d. An attempt by Rome to expand its territories

43. Who won the Second Punic War?

    a. The Carthaginians led by Hannibal

    b. The Romans led by Scipio Africanus

    c. Both sides agreed to a truce

    d. Neither side; it ended in a stalemate

44. How did Roman victories during the Third Punic War end Carthage's power?

a. The Romans destroyed most of its citizens with plague or famine

b. The Romans captured and enslaved many people

c. All of Carthage's buildings were burned down

d. Carthage was forced to sign a treaty that forfeited all its rights as an independent state

45. How did Rome gain control over its provinces in Spain and North Africa during the Punic Wars?

a. By winning decisive battles against Carthage on land and sea

b. Through diplomatic negotiations with local leaders

c. By establishing colonies and trading posts

d. Through harsh military occupations that suppressed any resistance

46. What was one consequence of Rome's victory in the Second Punic War?

a. It allowed Rome to expand the republic in western Europe

b. It caused Carthage to become a rival power again

c. It increased trade between Italy and Greece

d. It weakened Rome's political structure at home by increasing debt

47. Why was Carthage a threat to the Roman Republic?

a. It had plotted a revolution in Rome

b. It had invaded Roman territories before the Punic Wars

c. It held great economic influence in the Mediterranean

d. It had rapidly increased its military

48. How did Rome eventually defeat Hannibal during the Second Punic War?

a. By launching a counter-invasion into Spain

b. By cutting off his supplies and reinforcements from Carthage

c. Through a series of naval battles in the Mediterranean

d. By assassinating him

49. Who did the Roman Senate elect at times of crisis, such as war, to lead temporarily?

a. A praetor

b. The consul

c. A dictator

d. None of the above

50. How did Hannibal invade Italy and attack Rome?

a. He crossed the Alps and attacked from the north

b. He launched an offensive from Sicily

c. He landed near Rome with ships

d. None of the above

51. How did the Roman Republic eventually transition to an empire?

a. Julius Caesar overthrew it and declared himself emperor

b. The Senate voted in favor of a monarchy

c. It was invaded by outside forces

d. It evolved from its republican form over time

52. How long did Roman citizens serve as senators?

a. Eight years

b. Four years

c. Two years

d. For life

53. Which of these did not take place during the Roman Republic?

a. The Pyrrhic War

b. The Macedonian War

c. The Samnite War

d. None of the above

54. What policy did the Roman Republic adopt toward conquered nations?

a. Absorption, by allowing them to join and become citizens of Rome

b. Assimilation, by forcing their cultures to merge with that of Rome

c. Expansionism, by expanding its territories across other regions

d. Isolationism, keeping conquered nations separate from Roman society

55. Which of these was the decisive battle of the Second Punic War, ending in Rome's victory?

a. Canae

b. Zama

c. Panormus

d. None of the above

56. How many consuls served as chief magistrates in the Senate during the Roman Republic?

a. One

b. Two

c. Three

d. Four

57. What happened to Lucius Tarquiniius Superbus, the last king of Rome?

a. He was assassinated

b. He was forced into exile

c. He was swarmed by an angry mob in the streets

d. None of the above

58. What was the responsibility of the praetors in the Roman Senate?

a. To collect taxes

b. To raise armies

c. To organize yearly censuses

d. To lead the civil administration of justice

59. Who wrote *On Duties*, an important work outlining ethical behavior for Romans during this era?

a. Cicero

b. Livy

c. Virgil

d. Plutarch

60. What was the Roman Republic's primary goal in conducting foreign policy?

a. Expansion of its territories and resources

b. Trade with other civilizations

c. Maintenance of peaceful relations

d. Establishment of military alliances

ANSWERS

41. b. Carthage

42. a. Conflict over Sicily

43. b. The Romans led by Scipio Africanus

44. d. Carthage was forced to sign a treaty that forfeited all its rights as an independent state

45. a. By winning decisive battles against Carthage on land and sea

46. a. It allowed Rome to expand the republic in western Europe

47. c. Because it held great economic influence in the Mediterranean

48. b. By cutting off his supplies and reinforcements from Carthage

49. c. A dictator

50. a. He crossed the Alps and attacked from the north

51. a. Julius Caesar overthrew it and declared himself emperor

52. d. For life

53. d. None of the above

54. a. Absorption, by allowing them to join and become citizens of Rome

55. b. Zama

56. b. Two

57. b. He was forced into exile

58. d. To lead the civil administration of justice

59. a. Cicero

60. a. Expansion of its territories and resources

Julius Caesar and the Fall of the Roman Empire

Embark on a journey through the legendary life and untimely death of Julius Caesar, one of ancient Rome's most enduring historical figures. Unravel the mystery of Caesar's ascension to power, from his military conquests and political reforms to his eventual downfall. From his famous crossing of the Rubicon and his tumultuous alliance with Octavian and Antony to the assassination that shocked a nation, this chapter will test your ability to remember the finer details of one of ancient Rome's most well-known figures.

61. Who was Julius Caesar before he became emperor?

a. General and statesman

b. A Gallic rebel

c. Greek invader

d. None of the above

62. Julius Caesar was famously captured by pirates in what year?

a. 75 BCE

b. 27 BCE

c. 54 BCE

d. 64 CE

63. Which Roman political office was held by Julius Caesar before becoming dictator?

a. Tribunate

b. Consulate

c. Praetorship

d. Censor

64. Where did Caesar campaign before becoming emperor?

a. Greece

b. Germania

c. Gaul

d. North Africa

65. Who were the other two members of the Triumvirate, an informal political alliance among the Roman elites?

a. Pompey and Crassus

b. Pompey and Brutus

c. Brutus and Crassus

d. None of the above

66. Who became the main political rival of Caesar?

a. Mark Antony

b. Octavian

c. Brutus

d. Pompey

67. Where was Julius Caesar assassinated?

a. Rome

b. Alexandria

c. Philippi

d. Gaul

68. What year did Julius Caesar become dictator for life?

a. 44 BCE

b. 54 BCE

c. 27 BCE

d. 64 CE

69. When was Caesar proclaimed an enemy of the state by the Senate?

    a. 45 BCE

    b. 50 BCE

    c. 49 BCE

    d. 46 BCE

70. What transpired after Caesar's assassination in 44 BCE?

    a. Rome returned to a republic

    b. The Senate was dissolved

    c. A civil war broke out

    d. All of the above

71. Where did Caesar and his legions land during their first invasion of Britain?

    a. London

    b. Kent

    c. Cornwall

    d. Dover

72. In which battle did Crassus die?

    a. Rubicon River

    b. Pharsalus

    c. Carrhae

    d. None of the above

73. When did Caesar begin the invasion of Gaul?

    a. 60 BCE

    b. 59 BCE

    c. 58 BCE

    d. 57 BCE

74. What was the decisive battle of the Gallic Wars in 52 BCE that decided the fate of the war?

    a. Battle of the Vosges

    b. Battle of Atuatuci

    c. Battle of Avaricum

    d. Battle of Alesia

75. The migration of which of these tribes is thought to have triggered the outbreak of the Gallic Wars?

a. Suebi

b. Goths

c. Helvetii

d. Angles

76. What were some of the most important reforms enacted by Julius Caesar as dictator?

a. Abolition of slavery

b. Expansion of the Senate

c. Introduction of new coins

d. Reforms in taxation and public spending

77. Who did Caesar adopt as his son?

a. Mark Antony

b. Octavian

c. Caracalla

d. None of the above

78. What year marked an end to hostilities between Octavian and Antony after almost ten years of civil unrest?

a. 31 BCE

b. 44 BCE

c. 54 BCE

d. 27 CE

79. Why did Julius Caesar cross the Rubicon, which was considered a treasonous act?

a. To meet with Pompey

b. To free slaves

c. To gain military forces

d. To march on Rome

80. Who became the first emperor of Rome after Caesar?

a. Octavian

b. Nero

c. Mark Antony

d. Trajan

81. How many legions were under the command of Julius Caesar when he crossed the Rubicon?

 a. One legion

 b. Two legions

 c. Three legions

 d. Four legions

82. What was the Principate?

 a. The name of Caesar's most favorite army contingent

 b. An advisory body created by Octavian

 c. The form of Roman imperial government established under Octavian

 d. None of the above

83. What honorific title did Octavian adopt?

 a. Germanicus

 b. Augustus

 c. Caesaricus

 d. All of the above

84. What became Octavian's main basis for maintaining his power in Rome?

 a. A strong and loyal army

 b. Favors with the Senate

 c. His statesmanship

 d. None of the above

85. Who is the author of *Commentarii de Bello Civili*, which tells the story of the civil war between Caesar and Pompey?

 a. Virgil

 b. Livy

 c. Cicero

 d. Julius Caesar

ANSWERS

61. a. General and statesman

62. a. 75 BCE

63. b. Consulate

64. c. Gaul

65. a. Pompey and Crassus

66. d. Pompey

67. a. Rome

68. a. 44 BCE

69. c. 49 BCE

70. c. A civil war broke out

71. b. Kent

72. c. Carrhae

73. c. 58 BCE

74. d. Battle of Alesia

75. c. Helvetii

76. d. Reforms in taxation and public spending

77. b. Octavian

78. a. 31 BCE

79. d. To march on Rome

80. a. Octavian

81. a. One legion

82. c. The form of Roman imperial government established under Octavian

83. b. Augustus

84. a. A strong and loyal army

85. d. Julius Caesar

Augustus: Empire's Birth, Pax Romana, and Imperial Cult

(Octavian) Augustus, the founder of the Roman Empire, is credited with ushering in a form of government known as the Principate. He implemented numerous social and religious reforms that shaped Rome into a powerful state during his reign. Through military campaigns and civil law reforms, Augustus fostered peace while continuing to expand the empire's power abroad. His complex relationship between religion and politics enabled him to create loyalty among his citizens through temple construction, which incorporated imperial cults dedicated to himself. This chapter aims to explore how Augustus' consolidation of authority led him toward creating Pax Romana. You'll answer questions about imperial cults, militaristic campaigns, economic development strategies, and civic law implementations within ancient Roman societies under his rule.

86. In which naval battle did Augustus decisively defeat Mark Antony?

    a. Lepanto

    b. Actium

    c. Aegates

    d. None of the above

87. Which title of Emperor Octavian means "first citizen"?

    a. Princeps   c. Primis

    b. Augustus   d. Caesar

88. How did the imperial cult contribute to Augustus' consolidation of power?

    a. Through religious ceremonies and rituals to demonstrate loyalty

    b. By granting titles, honorifics, and money to supporters

    c. By reserving the title "Augustus" for him and his family

    d. None of the above

89. When did Octavian Augustus die?

    a. 12 CE

    b. 14 CE

    c. 20 CE

    d. 15 CE

90. What was the Praetorian Guard?

    a. An honorific title given to a group of senators during the empire

    b. An elite military unit established under Octavian Augustus

    c. A group of statesmen who aimed to restore the republic

    d. None of the above

91. What type of government did Augustus establish?

    a. A monarchy with himself as king

    b. An absolute dictatorship where he had complete control

    c. A republic resembling the Roman Republic

    d. A government dependent on trade and alliances

92. Augustus implemented various reforms, including introducing which of these?

    a. Public libraries

    b. A postal system

    c. A progressive tax system

    d. All of the above

93. What boosted tax revenues during the reign of Augustus?

    a. Free trade

    b. Imposition of a regular census

    c. Reduction in tax rates

    d. Direct collection of taxes by the emperor

94. What was not among the reforms of Augustus?

a. Abolition of slavery

b. Creation of a poll tax

c. Implementation of a new system of coinage

d. Creation of new political positions

95. Which of these regions was Rome unable to conquer under Augustus?

a. Iberia

b. Dalmatia

c. Noricum

d. Germania

96. What honorific title was awarded to Augustus in 2 BCE?

a. "Father of the Country"

b. "Bringer of Peace"

c. "First Ruler"

d. All of the above

97. What is the Pax Romana, or Roman Peace?

a. The name of the treaty that ended the civil war between Octavian and Mark Antony

b. The name given to the period of prosperity and relative stability during the first two centuries of the empire

c. A special military unit created by Augustus to protect the emperor

d. None of the above

98. What were among the reforms of Augustus?

a. Adoption of Christianity

b. Creation of local councils in the conquered provinces of the empire

c. Division of Italy into new administrative departments

d. Implementation of state-owned banks

99. Which civil institution was introduced in Rome during Augustus' rule?

a. A music library

b. Fire department

c. Trade union

d. All of the above

100. Who succeeded Augustus?

    a. Tiberius

    b. Nero

    c. Caligula

    d. Marcus Aurelius

101. When did Tiberius become princeps?

    a. 14 CE

    b. 18 CE

    c. 20 CE

    d. 22 CE

102. How did Tiberius compare with his predecessor?

    a. He participated in far more military campaigns

    b. He paid no attention to the needs of the citizens

    c. He was far more ruthless

    d. He was a less charismatic and competent as a ruler

103. Who was the adopted son of Tiberius?

    a. Livy

    b. Brutus

    c. Germanicus

    d. None of the above

104. Which political opponent of Tiberius was executed for treason in 31 CE?

    a. Nero Claudius Drusus

    b. Lucius Aelius Sejanus

    c. Germanicus

    d. None of the above

105. When did Tiberius die?

    a. 40 CE

    b. 45 CE

    c. 37 CE

    d. 39 CE

ANSWERS

86. b. Actium

87. a. Princeps

88. a. Through religious ceremonies and rituals to demonstrate loyalty

89. b. 14 CE

90. b. An elite military unit established by Octavian Augustus

91. b. An absolute dictatorship where he had complete control

92. d. All of the above

93. b. Imposition of a regular census

94. a. Abolition of slavery

95. d. Germania

96. a. "Father of the Country"

97. b. The name given to the period of prosperity and relative stability during the first two centuries of the empire

98. c. Division of Italy into new administrative departments

99. b. Fire department

100. a. Tiberius

101. a. 14 CE

102. d. He was less charismatic and competent as a ruler

103. c. Germanicus

104. b. Lucius Aelius Sejanus

105. c. 37 CE

From Tiberius to Nero's Reign

From the reign of Tiberius to Nero's eventual suicide, Rome was a vast and powerful empire. During this period, imperial governors held the title of "legate," while legions numbered over thirty. Rulers such as Claudius implemented important legislation and sought to expand Roman territories, while philosophers like Plato inspired famous figures, including Seneca and Lucan. Test your knowledge of how far ancient Rome's influence spread with this chapter's questions covering Tiberius to Nero's reign.

106. Who succeeded Tiberius as emperor of Rome?

    a. Caligula

    b. Augustus

    c. Claudius

    d. Nero

107. What was the title given to imperial governors in the provinces during this period?

    a. Dux

    b. Legate

    c. Magistrate

    d. Tribune

108. When did Nero become emperor?

    a. 49 CE

    b. 37 CE

    c. 25 CE

    d. 54 CE

109. **What event directly led to the end of Nero's rule and his suicide in 68 CE?**

   a. The Great Fire

   b. The Battle of Actium

   c. Uprising of Vespasian

   d. None of the above

110. **When did the Great Fire of Rome take place?**

   a. 60 CE

   b. 68 CE

   c. 64 CE

   d. None of the above

111. **Who was the predecessor of Nero as the emperor of Rome?**

   a. Tiberius

   b. Claudius

   c. Caligula

   d. Marcus Aurelius

112. **Who was Nero's tutor?**

   a. Aristotle

   b. Seneca the Younger

   c. Epictetus

   d. None of the above

113. **Which of these was one of Tiberius' most famous accomplishments as emperor?**

   a. The Battle of Actium

   b. Reform of the Senate

   c. Founding of the Praetorian Guard

   d. None of the above

114. **Who wrote the *Annals*, which detailed Tiberius' rule to Nero's accession to power?**

   a. Plutarch

   b. Tacitus

   c. Livy

   d. Suetonius

115. Who was the nephew of Claudius?

a. Tacitus

b. Caligula

c. Nero

d. Trajan

116. What was Claudius' profession before he became emperor?

a. Senator

b. Historian

c. Philosopher

d. None of the above

117. What was the name of Nero's first wife?

a. Poppaea Sabina

b. Claudia Octavia

c. Livia Drusilla

d. Agrippina Major

118. Who did Nero blame the Great Fire of Rome on?

a. The Senate

b. Etruscans

c. Christians

d. Claudius

119. What regional power did Rome come into conflict with during this era?

a. Gauls

b. Greeks

c. Jews

d. Parthians

120. Where did Rome mainly wish to expand during the reign of Nero?

a. Armenia

b. North Africa

c. Gaul

d. None of the above

121. How did Caligula die?

    a. He was assassinated

    b. He died from the wounds he had suffered in battle

    c. He fell off his horse and drowned in the river

    d. He died of old age

122. How many years did Nero rule as emperor?

    a. Fifteen years

    b. Thirteen years

    c. Eleven years

    d. Nine years

123. Which was the most populous province of Rome during this period?

    a. Egypt

    b. Asia Minor

    c. Gaul

    d. Italia

124. What was the name of Nero's mother?

    a. Agrippina the Younger

    b. Poppaea Sabina

    c. Octavia Minor

    d. Livia Drusilla

125. What did Nero use as an excuse to execute Seneca?

    a. He was plotting against him

    b. He refused to share his wealth

    c. He was spreading Christian propaganda

    d. None of the above

ANSWERS

106. a. Caligula

107. b. Legate

108. d. 54 CE

109. d. None of the above

110. c. 64 CE

111. b. Claudius

112. b. Seneca the Younger

113. d. None of the above

114. b. Tacitus

115. b. Caligula

116. b. Historian

117. b. Claudia Octavia

118. c. Christians

119. d. Parthians

120. a. Armenia

121. a. He was assassinated

122. b. Thirteen years

123. d. Italia

124. a. Agrippina the Younger

125. a. He was plotting against him

The Flavian Dynasty and the Rise of Christianity

The Flavian dynasty took the Roman Empire through a period of politic al, military, and cultural change. During this time, three emperors— Vespasian, Titus, and Domitian—guided the empire with their unique governing strategies and laid the foundations for future expansion. This chapter poses intriguing questions about these rulers who initiated monumental construction projects, shaped Christianity's emergence, furthered development in art, and captured foreign lands. Let's get started on our quest!

126. Who founded the Flavian dynasty?

    a. Claudius

    b. Nero

    c. Vespasian

    d. Diocletian

127. During which emperor's reign was Jerusalem destroyed and the temple of Jerusalem sacked in 70 CE?

    a. Vespasian

    b. Nerva

    c. Titus

    d. Trajan

128. Who oversaw the quelling of the Jewish rebellion that led to the siege of Jerusalem in this era?

a. Trajan

b. Titus

c. Marcus Aurelius

d. None of the above

129. When did Domitian become an emperor after his brother's death?

a. 81 CE

b. 69 BCE

c. 96 CE

d. 79 CE

130. How many emperors were in the Flavian dynasty?

a. Two

b. Three

c. Four

d. Five

131. Who was Titus?

a. Vespasian's father

b. A local military general from Palestine

c. Vespasian's son

d. None of the above

132. Which event marked the end of the Flavian dynasty?

a. Assassination of Domitian

b. Death of Titus

c. Defeat against the Parthians

d. None of the above

133. How were Domitian and Titus related?

a. They were father and son

b. They were brothers

c. They weren't related

d. None of the above

134. When was Domitian assassinated by a conspiracy?

    a. 90 CE

    b. 92 CE

    c. 95 CE

    d. 96 CE

135. Under whose reign was the Colosseum in Rome built?

    a. Vespasian

    b. Titus

    c. Domitian

    d. None of the above

136. What was the main purpose of the Colosseum?

    a. It was an open theater

    b. It was an arena for gladiatorial fights

    c. It was a forum for political rallies

    d. None of the above

137. How did Vespasian become emperor?

    a. He inherited it from his father

    b. He usurped the throne by killing the previous emperor

    c. He was proclaimed so by the eastern legions

    d. None of the above

138. Who wrote *The Jewish War*, an account of the Jews' revolt against the Romans during the Flavian dynasty?

    a. Tacitus

    b. Plutarch

    c. Suetonius

    d. Flavius Josephus

139. Which emperor of the Flavian dynasty was chiefly responsible for the Roman expansion in Britain?

    a. Vespasian

    b. Titus

    c. Domitian

    d. Nerva

140. What name is given to the period of 68-69 CE, before the proclamation of Vespasian as emperor?

a. The Dark Year

b. The Year of the Four Emperors

c. The Year of Peace

d. None of the above

141. Who was the emperor murdered by Vespasian's troops in 69 CE, before Vespasian became emperor?

a. Otho

b. Nerva

c. Vitellius

d. Galba

142. What major accomplishments attributed to Vespasian and his sons helped shape the Roman Empire under their rule?

a. Expansion in Britain, Asia Minor, and the eastern Mediterranean

b. Improvement in public services such as the construction of roads and aqueducts

c. Promotion of pagan religion through temple building projects

d. All of the above

143. Who succeeded Domitian after his assassination in 96 CE?

a. Nerva

b. Trajan

c. Titus

d. Diocletian

144. Why was Domitian disfavored by the Senate?

a. He was a drunkard

b. He had increased taxes

c. He was an authoritarian ruler

d. All of the above

145. What position did Nerva hold before he became the emperor?

a. Domitian's advisor

b. Consul

c. Legate of Britain

d. None of the above

ANSWERS

126. c. Vespasian

127. a. Vespasian

128. b. Titus

129. a. 81 CE

130. b. Three

131. c. Vespasian's son

132. a. Assassination of Domitian

133. b. They were brothers

134. d. 96 CE

135. a. Vespasian

136. b. It was an arena for gladiatorial fights

137. c. He was proclaimed so by the Eastern legions

138. d. Flavius Josephus

139. a. Vespasian

140. b. The Year of the Four Emperors

141. c. Vitellius

142. d. All of the above

143. a. Nerva

144. c. He was an authoritarian ruler

145. a. Domitian's advisor

Five Good Emperors: Nerva, Trajan, Hadrian, Antoninus Pius, and Marcus Aurelius

Welcome to our chapter about the Five Good Emperors. These five outstanding Roman leaders are revered for the contributions each made during his respective reign. We will compare their extraordinary accomplishments and discover who was considered the most successful emperor among them. Each of these rulers implemented progressive social reforms that left a lasting impact on imperial Rome while establishing many public works like aqueducts and libraries. Although they ruled nearly two thousand years ago, we can still look back today and marvel at how influential these Five Good Emperors were in shaping ancient history.

146. Who was the first of the Five Good Emperors?

a. Nerva

b. Trajan

c. Hadrian

d. Antoninus Pius

147. Which city did Hadrian famously rebuild and rename after a significant rebellion?

a. Carthage

b. Alexandria

c. Jerusalem

d. Byzantium

148. Who was considered an excellent philosopher-emperor, known for writing *Meditations*?

    a. Nerva

    b. Trajan

    c. Hadrian

    d. Marcus Aurelius

149. How did Nerva die?

    a. Natural causes

    b. Poisoning

    c. He was assassinated

    d. None of the above

150. When did Trajan become emperor?

    a. 95 CE

    b. 98 CE

    c. 100 CE

    d. None of the above

151. Of what relation was Trajan to Nerva?

    a. He was his brother

    b. He was his uncle

    c. He was his advisor

    d. He was his adopted son

152. What was significant about Nerva's reign as emperor that distinguished him from his predecessors?

    a. He granted citizenship to all Roman citizens

    b. He made Christianity legal in Rome

    c. He abolished slavery

    d. None of the above

153. When did Trajan die?

    a. 114 CE

    b. 115 CE

    c. 116 CE

    d. 117 CE

154. Under which emperor did Rome reach its greatest extent in terms of territory?

a. Nerva

b. Trajan

c. Hadrian

d. Marcus Aurelius

155. Who succeeded Trajan as the next emperor?

a. Hadrian

b. Marcus Aurelius

c. Antoninus Pius

d. Commodus

156. What is not considered an accomplishment of Antoninus Pius?

a. Offensives in southern Scotland

b. Legal reform

c. Reformation of the tax system

d. Invasion and annexation of Gaul

157. When did the Antonine Plague break out in Rome?

a. 155 CE

b. 165 CE

c. 175 CE

d. None of the above

158. Who was the Roman emperor by the time the Antonine Plague broke out?

a. Hadrian

b. Trajan

c. Antoninus Pius

d. Marcus Aurelius

159. Which of the Five Good Emperors has an equestrian statue of himself in Rome?

a. Nerva

b. Marcus Aurelius

c. Trajan

d. Antoninus Pius

160. What is one characteristic that all five of these rulers had in common?

a. They were all philosophers

b. They tolerated Christianity

c. They reigned for at least fifty years

d. None of the above

161. Which of these emperors managed to conquer the province of Dacia for the Roman Empire?

a. Nerva

b. Trajan

c. Hadrian

d. Antoninus Pius

162. Which of these emperors is responsible for the reconstruction and renovation of the Circus Maximus theater in Rome?

a. Nerva

b. Trajan

c. Hadrian

d. Marcus Aurelius

163. Which of these emperors corresponded with Pliny the Younger regarding the persecution of Christians in Asia Minor during his reign?

a. Nerva

b. Trajan

c. Hadrian

d. Marcus Aurelius

164. Who succeeded Marcus Aurelius as the next emperor?

a. Commodus

b. Lucius Verus

c. Diocletian

d. None of the above

165. Which of the emperors constructed the Temple of Venus and Roma, thought to have been the largest temple in ancient Rome?

a. Nerva

b. Trajan

c. Hadrian

d. Marcus Aurelius

166. Historians consider Rome's decline to have begun under which of these emperors?

a. Marcus Aurelius

b. Commodus

c. Nerva

d. Trajan

167. Whose work is Trajan's "Commentary on the Dacian Wars" modeled after?

a. Octavian

b. Virgil

c. Julius Caesar

d. Plutarch

168. During whose reign did Rome wage the Marcomannic Wars?

a. Trajan

b. Hadrian

c. Marcus Aurelius

d. Nerva

169. Who emerged victorious from the Marcomannic Wars?

a. Rome

b. Parthia

c. The Marcomanni

d. None of the above

170. What caused the Roman-Parthian War of 161-166 CE?

a. Parthian rebellion

b. Assassination of a Roman senator

c. Invasion of Armenia by Rome

d. Invasion of Armenia by Parthia

ANSWERS

146. a. Nerva

147. c. Jerusalem

148. d. Marcus Aurelius

149. a. Natural causes

150. b. 98 CE

151. d. He was his adopted son

152. d. None of the above

153. d. 117 CE

154. b. Trajan

155. a. Hadrian

156. d. Invasion and annexation of Gaul

157. b. 165 CE

158. d. Marcus Aurelius

159. b. Marcus Aurelius

160. d. None of the above

161. b. Trajan

162. b. Trajan

163. b. Trajan

164. a. Commodus

165. c. Hadrian

166. b. Commodus

167. c. Julius Caesar

168. c. Marcus Aurelius

169. a. Rome

170. d. Invasion of Armenia by Parthia

Severan Dynasty, Crisis of the Third Century, and Diocletian's Reforms

Are you ready to explore the incredible history of ancient Rome's famed Severan dynasty, the dramatic Crisis of the Third Century, and Diocletian's far-reaching reforms? These twenty questions will challenge your knowledge of this fascinating era in Roman history. From who established the Severan dynasty to who put a stop to the Third Century Crisis, each answer is a piece to understanding the complexity of power shifts that shaped Roman life for centuries. Brush up on your trivia skills as we dive into this remarkable period with its notable emperors and events.

171. Who was the founder of the Severan dynasty?

 a. Septimius Severus

 b. Diocletian

 c. Constantine I

 d. Marcus Aurelius

172. In what year did the Crisis of the Third Century begin?

 a. 241 CE

 b. 204 CE

 c. 235 CE

 d. 324 CE

173. Into how many parts did the Roman Empire split during the crisis?

a. One

b. Two

c. Three

d. Four

174. What reforms did Diocletian introduce to restore order and stability in Rome?

a. Creation of new administrative regions

b. Abolition of slavery

c. Toleration of Christianity

d. All the above

175. Who was the co-emperor with Diocletian?

a. Maximian

b. Constantius Chlorus

c. Galerius

d. Claudius Gothicus

176. During which century did most members of the Severan dynasty rule?

a. Second century CE

b. Third century CE

c. Fourth century CE

d. Fifth century CE

177. Who succeeded Septimus Severus as emperor?

a. Caracalla

b. Diocletian and Caracalla

c. Geta and Caracalla

d. Geta

178. What was the Tetrarchy?

a. A new form of governance in Roman Asia Minor

b. A new administrative division of Roman territories into four parts

c. A Christian state that briefly existed in the Roman Empire

d. None of the above

179. In what year did Emperor Elagabalus come to power during the Severan dynasty?

a. 218 CE

b. 220 CE

c. 226 CE

d. 252 CE

180. Which emperor is responsible for achieving successive military victories that resulted in the end of the Crisis of the Third Century?

a. Septimus Severus

b. Diocletian

c. Aurelian

d. Caracalla

181. Which emperor introduced an edict that granted citizenship to all free men of Rome in 212 CE?

a. Diocletian

b. Elagabalus

c. Geta

d. Caracalla

182. What was Diocletian's main goal when he introduced his reforms in 284 CE?

a. To restore order to Rome after a long civil war

b. To make the empire easier to govern

c. To consolidate military power in the empire

d. All of the above

183. Who succeeded Elagabalus as Roman emperor after his assassination in 222 CE?

a. Severus Alexander

b. Caracalla

c. Maximinus II

d. Claudius Gothicus

184. In what year did Septimius Severus become emperor?

a. 193 CE

b. 197 CE

c. 201 CE

d. 225 CE

185. Which of these emperors is infamous for his persecution of Christians?

    a. Caracalla

    b. Diocletian

    c. Geta

    d. Septimus Severus

186. How did Caracalla die?

    a. Natural causes

    b. Illness

    c. Assassination

    d. None of the above

187. Which emperor managed to sack the Parthian capital of Ctesiphon in 197 CE?

    a. Septimus Severus

    b. Caracalla

    c. Geta

    d. None of the above

188. Who succeeded Caracalla as emperor after his assassination in 217 CE?

    a. Macrinus

    b. Elagabalus

    c. Alexander Severus

    d. Maximinus II

189. What year did Emperor Caracalla's reign begin?

    a. 197 CE

    b. 211 CE

    c. 213 CE

    d. 219 CE

190. Who were the two Caesars that assisted the two Augusti in ruling the empire in the first iteration of the Tetrarchy?

    a. Macrinus and Elagabalus

    b. Maximinus II and Galerius

    c. Severus Alexander and Diocletian

    d. Constantius Chlorus and Galerius

191. Who are depicted on the sculpture of the Four Tetrarchs?

    a. Nero, Diocletian, Maximian, Galerius

    b. Diocletian, Maximian, Galerius, and Constantius

    c. Theodosius, Diocletian, Constantine, Marcus Aurelius

    d. None of the above

192. Which of these was not one of the capitals of the Tetrarchy?

    a. Trier

    b. Milan

    c. Nicomedia

    d. Rome

193. Where is the Triumphal Arch of the Tetrarchy located?

    a. Algeria

    b. Tunisia

    c. Libya

    d. Egypt

194. Who built a namesake rotunda in Thessaloniki?

    a. Maximian

    b. Galerius

    c. Diocletian

    d. Constantine

195. Before becoming emperor himself, under which Roman emperor did Diocletian serve as a cavalry commander?

    a. Carus

    b. Probus

    c. Valentinian

    d. None of the above

ANSWERS

171. a. Septimius Severus

172. c. 235 CE

173. c. Three

174. a. Creation of new administrative regions

175. a. Maximian

176. b. Third century CE

177. c. Geta and Caracalla

178. b. A new administrative division of Roman territories into four parts

179. a. 218 CE

180. c. Aurelian

181. d. Caracalla

182. d. All of the above

183. a. Severus Alexander

184. a. 193 CE

185. b. Diocletian

186. c. Assassination

187. a. Septimus Severus

188. a. Macrinus

189. b. 211 CE

190. d. Constantius and Galerius

191. b. Diocletian, Maximian, Galerius, Constantius

192. d. Rome

193. b. Tunisia

194. b. Galerius

195. a. Carus

Constantine I: Christianization of Rome

Emperor Constantine I is one of the most influential figures in ancient Rome. He led a revolution that changed Roman society forever by promoting religious tolerance and issuing his Edict of Milan. Questions in this chapter will explore Constantine I's role in Christianizing Rome, the impact of his conversion and the revolution it caused, as well as details about the Edict of Milan, Council of Nicaea, and the circumstances around Constantine's reign.

196. How did Constantine I help spread Christianity throughout ancient Rome?

a. By converting and providing an example

b. By encouraging people to convert to Christianity and offering them incentives for doing so

c. By establishing churches across different cities

d. All of the above

197. After which of the following did Emperor Constantine convert to Christianity?

a. The Siege of Ravenna

b. The adoption of paganism

c. The construction of Constantinople's walls

d. The Battle of Milvian Bridge

198. Which statement best describes how religion impacted the lives of Romans during this period?

a. Religion was irrelevant to Roman life

b. Paganism was the only religion practiced in the empire

c. Christianity had become a major part of Roman culture

d. All religious practices were prohibited by law

199. Which edict did Constantine issue after his conversion to Christianity in 313 CE?

a. The Edict of Nicaea

b. The Edict of Milan

c. The Edict of Rome

d. None of the above

200. How did Constantine's edict affect paganism within ancient Rome?

a. It outlawed all forms of pagan worship

b. It became more popular than ever before

c. It remained an accepted form of belief but lost much political power

d. It spread its influence across different cities

201. In addition to the promotion of Christianity, which of these is among the major decisions of Constantine's reign?

a. The reorganization of the army in Gaul and Britain

b. The founding of Constantinople

c. The debasing of coinage to combat inflation

d. None of the above

202. Where was Constantine acclaimed as Augustus by his forces in 306 CE?

a. Britain

b. Spain

c. Egypt

d. Asia Minor

203. According to the Edict of Milan, what punishment was imposed on anyone found guilty of persecuting Christians?

a. Fines and confiscation

b. Exile from Rome

c. Execution

d. Imprisonment

204. When did Constantine die?

a. 337 CE

b. 338 CE

c. 339 CE

d. 340 CE

205. When was the Council of Nicaea held?

a. 331 CE

b. 316 CE

c. 325 CE

d. 330 CE

206. What was discussed at the Council of Nicaea?

a. Fate of the Roman Empire

b. Role of the emperor in the Christian church

c. Important doctrinal matters of Christianity

d. Constantine's succession

207. What was the name of the site of the old Greek city upon which Constantinople was founded?

a. Tripoli

b. Antioch

c. Trebizond

d. Byzantium

208. Which emperor proclaimed Christianity as the official religion of the Roman Empire?

a. Maximian

b. Theodosius

c. Constantine

d. Constantine II

209. When was Christianity proclaimed the official religion of the Roman Empire?

a. 358 CE

b. 379 CE

c. 380 CE

d. 383 CE

210. Which edict proclaimed Christianity as the official religion of the Roman Empire?

a. Edict of Nicaea

b. Edict of Thessalonica

c. Edict of Constantinople

d. Edict of Ravenna

211. How did Christians in Rome react to the Edict of Milan?

a. They were pleased and thankful, as they could now practice their faith openly

b. They opposed it due to its acceptance of paganism

c. They felt betrayed since it also granted freedom of worship to pagans

d. None of the above

212. Where did Rome focus on expansion during the reign of Constantine I?

a. Armenia and the Caucasus

b. Northern Gaul

c. Arabia

d. None of the above

213. When did Constantine I become the sole ruler of the Roman Empire?

a. 314 CE

b. 326 CE

c. 324 CE

d. None of the above

214. Which of these rival emperors did Constantine have to defeat to become the sole emperor?

a. Maximinus II

b. Diocletian

c. Licinius

d. All of them

215. What was the main purpose of the Edict of Milan issued in 313 CE?

a. To make Christianity the official religion of the Roman Empire

b. To grant religious tolerance to all faiths and restore confiscated property to Christians

c. To abolish the Roman Senate and centralize imperial power

d. To impose new taxes on pagan temples and shrines

196. d. All of the above

197. d. The Battle of Milvian Bridge

198. d. Christianity had become a major part of Roman culture

199. b. The Edict of Milan

200. c. It remained an accepted form of belief but lost much political power

201. b. The founding of Constantinople

202. a. Britain

203. d. Fines and confiscation

204. a. 337 CE

205. c. 325 CE

206. c. Important doctrinal matters of Christianity

207. d. Byzantium

208. b. Theodosius

209. c. 380 CE

210. b. Edict of Thessalonica

211. a. They were pleased and thankful, as they could now practice their faith openly

212. a. Armenia and the Caucasus

213. c. 324 CE

214. c. Licinius

215. b. To grant religious tolerance to all faiths and restore confiscated property to Christians

Fall of the Western Roman Empire

Witness the fall of one of the greatest empires in history: the Western Roman Empire. Join us as we explore this pivotal event through trivia questions that examine two centuries when a Germanic leader overthrew the Roman emperor and established his kingdom in Italy. Explore how Emperor Honorius tried to address barbarian invasions and uncover details about Alaric, the last emperor's residency, the role played by the Roman Senate, and the length of the last emperor's reign until his death. Experience it all with our ancient Rome trivia chapter on the fall of the Western Roman Empire.

216. What year marked the fall of the Western Roman Empire?

　　a. 466 CE

　　b. 476 CE

　　c. 614 CE

　　d. 717 CE

217. Who was the last emperor of Western Rome?

　　a. Constantine I

　　b. Julius Caesar

　　c. Romulus Augustus

　　d. Odoacer

218. Where did Emperor Romulus Augustulus reside when he abdicated his throne in 476 CE?

a. Ravenna

b. Milan

c. Campania

d. Rome

219. Which Germanic tribe is credited with overthrowing the Western Roman Empire and establishing its kingdom in Italy?

a. Visigoths

b. Ostrogoths

c. Franks

d. None of the above

220. Who was king of the Visigoths from 395 to 410 CE?

a. Theodosius

b. Alaric

c. Thadeus

d. None of the above

221. What event out of these contributed to the fall of the Western Roman Empire?

a. Barbarian invasions

b. The Great Fire of Rome

c. Civil war in Italy

d. Assassination of the Eastern Roman emperor

222. What did Emperor Honorius do to address barbarian invasions?

a. He negotiated peace treaties with them

b. He hired mercenaries from other regions

c. He built fortified walls around cities

d. He increased taxes

223. Who was the son of Theodosius I, the emperor of Western Rome after his father's death?

a. Arcadius

b. Honorius

c. Theodosius II

d. Romulus Augustus

224. Who was proclaimed Eastern Roman emperor after 476 CE?

a. Zeno

b. Romulus Augustulus

c. Leo I

d. Julius Nepos

225. When did the Vandals sack Rome?

a. 410 CE

b. 395 CE

c. 476 CE

d. 455 CE

226. What was the capital of the Visigothic Kingdom in the late fourth century?

a. Rome

b. Toulouse

c. Ravenna

d. Milan

227. How old was Emperor Romulus Augustus when he was deposed by Odoacer in 476 CE?

a. Fourteen

b. Twenty-four

c. Ten

d. Six

228. Why did a large number of Goths migrate into the territories of the Roman Empire?

a. They had exhausted their land

b. They were fleeing from the Hunnic invaders

c. They suffered from an ecological disaster

d. They were promised good living conditions in Rome

229. When did the Visigoths sack Rome?

a. 433 CE

b. 412 CE

c. 410 CE

d. 455 CE

230. Which areas remained under the control of Eastern Roman emperors after 476 CE?

a. North Africa

b. Italy

c. France

d. Egypt

231. When did Ravenna become the capital of the Western Roman Empire?

a. 400 CE

b. 402 CE

c. 410 CE

d. 424 CE

232. What happened to Romulus Augustulus after he abdicated his throne in 476 CE?

a. He was exiled from Rome

b. He was appointed as the Eastern Roman emperor

c. He was executed by Odoacer

d. None of the above

233. How did the Romans attempt to address the barbarian invasions?

a. They tried to ally with some barbarians

b. They attempted to negotiate peace

c. They attacked the barbarians to keep them out

d. All of the above

234. Which of these tribes did not migrate to Britain after the fall of the Western Roman Empire?

a. Angles

b. Saxons

c. Jutes

d. Goths

235. Until when did the Eastern Roman Empire survive after 476 CE?

a. 1202 CE

b. 800 CE

c. 1453 CE

d. 1121 CE

236. Which power replaced Parthia as the main rival of Rome in the east in the late third to early fourth centuries?

a. Arabia

b. Sassanid Persia

c. Armenia

d. None of the above

237. When did the Battle of Samarra take place?

a. 303 CE

b. 363 CE

c. 389 CE

d. 376 CE

238. How did Emperor Valens die in 378 CE?

a. From an illness

b. Natural causes

c. In battle

d. None of the above

239. Who replaced Valens as emperor in 379 CE?

a. Theodosius

b. Trajan

c. Julian

d. Geta

240. Which general tried to unite the Eastern and Western Roman Empire in 408 CE?

a. Pliny the Elder

b. Stilicho

c. Orestes

d. Maximilian

241. When was the empire finally divided into eastern and western halves?

a. 399 CE

b. 403 CE

c. 407 CE

d. 395 CE

242. Around which city did Theodosius construct the famous walls?

a. Rome

b. London

c. Constantinople

d. Jerusalem

243. Which of Theodosius' sons inherited the Western Roman Empire in 395 CE?

a. Arcadius

b. Honorius

c. Titus

d. None of the above

244. The fall of Rome marks the beginning of which historical era?

a. Classical antiquity

b. Baroque

c. Middle Ages

d. Post-modernism

245. What is another name used to refer to the Eastern Roman Empire?

a. Constantinople Empire

b. Byzantine Empire

c. Late Roman Empire

d. All of the above

ANSWERS

216. b. 476 CE
217. c. Romulus Augustus
218. c. Campania
219. b. Ostrogoths
220. b. Alaric
221. a. Barbarian invasions
222. b. He hired mercenaries from other regions
223. b. Honorius
224. a. Zeno
225. d. 455 CE
226. b. Toulouse
227. a. Fourteen
228. b. They were fleeing from the Hunnic invaders
229. c. 410 CE
230. d. Egypt
231. b. 402 CE
232. a. He was exiled from Rome
233. d. All of the above
234. d. Goths
235. c. 1453 CE
236. b. Sassanid Persia
237. b. 363 CE
238. c. In battle
239. a. Theodosius
240. b. Stilicho
241. d. 395 CE
242. c. Constantinople
243. b. Honorius
244. c. Middle Ages
245. b. Byzantine Empire

Mythology

Explore the depths of ancient Roman mythology and culture with this collection of ancient Rome history trivia questions. Immerse yourself in finding out who Vulcan's wife was or who the three sisters known as "the Fates" were. Uncover which goddess did not have her own temple, decipher Apollo's nine muses, and discover who is often referred to as "The Lightbringer." Challenge your knowledge of many gods, goddesses, and symbols from the original pantheon that still resonate today. With questions ranging from identifying Jupiter's thunderbolt to discovering Janus' two-faced purpose, find out how much you know about ancient Roman mythology.

246. What is the weapon of Jupiter in Roman mythology?

a. Thunderbolt

b. Trident

c. Hammer

d. Whip

247. How many major gods and goddesses were part of the original pantheon of ancient Rome?

a. Eight

b. Twelve

c. Sixteen

d. Twenty

248. Who is known as the god/goddess of wine, agriculture, fertility, and ritual madness in Roman mythology?

a. Mars

b. Bacchus

c. Apollo

d. Minerva

249. Who was Vulcan's wife in Roman mythology?

a. Juno

b. Minerva

c. Venus

d. Diana

250. What is the name of the Roman god/goddess of wisdom and magic?

a. Apollo

b. Mars

c. Mercury

d. Minerva

251. Who was Neptune's brother in Roman mythology?

a. Mars

b. Jupiter

c. Saturn

d. Ares

252. Who were the three sisters known as "the Fates" in ancient Rome's mythology?

a. The Muses

b. Norns

c. Graces

d. The Parcae

253. Who is Saturn in Roman mythology?

a. The father of Jupiter, Neptune, and Pluto

b. The sister of Venus

c. The god of the underworld

d. The brother of Mars

254. Which of these goddesses did not have her own temple in ancient Rome?

a. Isis

b. Venus

c. Athena

d. Juno

255. What is the name of the Roman goddess of war?

a. Bellona

b. Mars

c. Minerva

d. Diana

256. Who was known as the god of fire in ancient Rome's mythology?

a. Vulcan

b. Jupiter

c. Pluto

d. Mars

257. Who was the god of war in Roman mythology?

a. Ares

b. Neptune

c. Mars

d. Pluto

258. Which ancient civilization's mythology influenced Rome's most heavily?

a. Sumer

b. Egypt

c. Greece

d. Carthage

259. How many horses pulled Helios' chariot in ancient Rome's mythology?

a. Four

b. Six

c. Eight

d. Ten

260. Who is the Roman goddess of wild animals and hunting in Roman mythology?

a. Juno

b. Minerva

c. Venus

d. Diana

261. Who was the goddess of justice in Roman mythology?

a. Liberta

b. Justitia

c. Diana

d. Minerva

262. Who was known as the god of the sea in ancient Rome's mythology?

a. Vulcan

b. Jupiter

c. Neptune

d. Mars

263. Who was the chief deity in Roman mythology?

a. Apollo

b. Saturn

c. Jupiter

d. Pluto

264. Who is the Roman goddess of marriage and childbirth?

a. Juno

b. Minerva

c. Venus

d. Diana

265. What is the Roman god Vulcan's symbol?

a. Hammer and anvil

b. Lightning bolt

c. Trident

d. Laurel wreath

266. Who is the Roman god of the forests and fields?

a. Juno

b. Cybede

c. Faunus

d. Diana

267. Who is Fortuna in Roman mythology?

a. The goddess of wealth

b. The god of philosophy

c. The goddess of luck

d. None of the above

268. Who is the counterpart of the Greek god Poseidon in Roman mythology?

a. Vulcan

b. Jupiter

c. Neptune

d. Mars

269. Who is the father of Bacchus in Roman mythology?

a. Apollo

b. Saturn

c. Pluto

d. Jupiter

270. What was the sacred animal of the goddess Juno?

a. Goat

b. Peacock

c. Cat

d. Swan

246. a. Thunderbolt

247. b. Twelve

248. b. Bacchus

249. c. Venus

250. d. Minerva

251. b. Jupiter

252. d. The Parcae

253. a. The father of Jupiter, Neptune, and Pluto

254. c. Athena

255. a. Bellona

256. a. Vulcan

257. c. Mars

258. c. Greece

259. a. Four

260. d. Diana

261. b. Justitia

262. c. Neptune

263. c. Jupiter

264. a. Juno

265. a. Hammer and anvil

266. c. Faunus

267. c. The goddess of luck

268. c. Neptune

269. d. Jupiter

270. b. Peacock

Literature, Poetry, and Music

Explore the great accomplishments of ancient Rome in literature, poetry, and music with this chapter of *Ancient Rome Trivia*. From the works of Virgil to Horace's Roman poems, they have left an enduring mark on civilization. Learn about the stunningly intricate meters for Latin poems and the dramatic performances that inspire audiences centuries later. Delve into critical questions like these: What does carpe diem mean? Who wrote *Eclogues*? Get ready to impress your friends by discovering how much you can learn about Roman culture from two thousand years ago.

271. Approximately how long did it take to compose the *Aeneid*?

    a. Eleven years

    b. Fifteen years

    c. Twenty years

    d. Twenty-five years

272. Who was known for his satirical poems that mocked Roman society and politics?

    a. Propertius

    b. Juvenal

    c. Tibullus

    d. Lucretius

273. What is the name of the Roman goddess associated with music?

a. Juno

b. Venus

c. Apollo

d. Diana

274. Who wrote the *Eclogues*, a collection of pastoral poetry set in ancient Italy?

a. Virgil

b. Horace

c. Catullus

d. Plautus

275. How many books are included in the *Aeneid*?

a. Eight

b. Ten

c. Twelve

d. Fifteen

276. How did ancient Romans use singing as part of their culture and religion?

a. To entertain the gods and goddesses during festivals

b. As an offering to their ancestors on special occasions

c. During military gatherings or battles for motivation

d. All of the above

277. In what language were the earliest historical accounts of ancient Rome written?

a. Latin

b. Greek

c. Etruscan

d. Gaelic

278. What does *carpe diem* mean in Latin poetry from ancient Rome?

a. Be happy today

b. Seize the day

c. Live for tomorrow

d. Learn from yesterday

279. Which Roman poet is the main character of Dante's *Divine Comedy*?

   a. Virgil

   b. Ovid

   c. Horace

   d. Seneca

280. Where did ancient Romans often perform their plays and concerts?

   a. In public squares

   b. In amphitheaters

   c. In temples or shrines

   d. In colosseums

281. Who was the emperor during the time of Ovid?

   a. Augustus

   b. Theodosius

   c. Constantine

   d. Nero

282. Who wrote *The Art of Poetry* (*Ars Poetica*), a treatise on poetics according to classical principles?

   a. Virgil

   b. Horace

   c. Catullus

   d. Plautus

283. How many books make up Ovid's *Amores*?

   a. Five

   b. Seven

   c. Fifteen

   d. Three

284. What type of drama was most popular among the ancient Romans?

   a. Opera

   b. Tragedy

   c. Burlesque

   d. Melodrama

285. Which Roman poet was exiled by Emperor Augustus, likely because of his poem *Ars Amatoria* ("The Art of Love")?

a. Virgil

b. Horace

c. Ovid

d. Martial

286. What does *Ars Amatoria* mean?

a. The Art of Love

b. A Guide to Love

c. The Art of Poetry

d. A Guide to Friendship

287. What instrument was most commonly used in ancient Roman music performances and military ceremonies?

a. Lyre

b. Cithara

c. Tuba

d. Aulos

271. a. Eleven years

272. b. Juvenal

273. c. Apollo

274. a. Virgil

275. c. Twelve

276. d. All of the above

277. b. Greek

278. b. Seize the day

279. a. Virgil

280. b. In amphitheaters

281. a. Augustus

282. b. Horace

283. d. Three

284. b. Tragedy

285. c. Ovid

286. a. The Art of Love

287. c. Tuba

Art and Architecture

Discover the answers to these intriguing questions about art, architecture, and monuments in ancient Rome. From towering columns to colorful public murals, explore how the Romans used their creativity for the commemoration of history and display of power. Travel back in time with us as we reveal why some structures were built, what materials were used, and what construction techniques were employed. Learn why sculptures depict certain figures or gods and who is responsible for popular works such as the Pantheon or Colosseum, still admired today. Unlock the secrets of this fascinating civilization through ancient Rome trivia.

288. What was one purpose the Romans had for building monuments and public buildings?

a. To commemorate important events in their history

b. To show off how wealthy they were

c. To create a sense of community among citizens

d. All of the above

289. What are some common features found in ancient Roman artworks?

a. Tall, slim figures with realistic proportions

b. Bright colors and ornate patterns

c. Building scenes or natural landscapes

d. None of the above

290. Which type of material was used to build many ancient structures such as aqueducts and roads?

a. Clay bricks

b. Wood

c. Granite

d. Stone blocks

291. Which material had Rome utilized extensively since ca. 600 BCE in its building projects?

a. Red clay

b. Concrete

c. Granite

d. None of the above

292. Which of the following emperors oversaw the construction of the Pantheon in Rome?

a. Octavian Augustus

b. Diocletian

c. Nero

d. Hadrian

293. During whose reign (among others) was the Arena of Nîmes, located in Nîmes, France, constructed?

a. Hadrian

b. Octavian

c. Trajan

d. Nero

294. Which emperor constructed a victory arch in Benevento in 114-117 CE?

a. Hadrian

b. Trajan

c. Caligula

d. None of the above

295. What are some unique features found on many buildings from this period such as baths or villas?

a. Courtyards surrounded by colonnades

b. Vaults supported by barrel arches

c. Niches filled with statues

d. All of the above

296. Where is the Arch of Septimius Severus located?

a. Ravenna

b. Athens

c. Rome

d. Toulouse

297. How did Roman sculptors create more realistic figures when creating statues, busts, or relief carvings?

a. By using marble as their primary material

b. By adding subtle details such as drapery folds

c. By including facial expressions in figures

d. All of the above

298. Who wrote *Naturalis Historia* (Natural History), considered one of the first encyclopedias?

a. Pliny

b. Plutarch

c. Marcus Aurelius

d. Virgil

299. Trajan's Column features a narrative relief sculpture depicting scenes from which wars?

a. Parthian Wars

b. Dacian Wars

c. Second Civil War

d. All of the above

300. What was the Altar of Augustan Peace, commissioned by the Senate in the first century CE, dedicated to?

a. Octavian's succession as ruler

b. Achievements of the Pax Romana

c. Harmony between the Senate and the emperor

d. Octavian Augustus' name

301. What type of structure was used to transport water across long distances for public use in ancient Rome?

a. Reservoirs

b. Aqueducts

c. Tunnels

d. Bridges

302. What is considered the oldest bridge built in ancient Rome around the sixth century BCE?

a. Pons Sublicius

b. Pons Fabricius

c. Ponte Milvio

d. Pont du Gard

303. In what year was the Colosseum completed?

a. 72 CE

b. 78 CE

c. 80 CE

d. 88 CE

304. In which city is the Arch of Constantine located?

a. Ravenna

b. Constantinople

c. Jerusalem

d. Rome

305. During whose reign did ancient Roman art reach its peak in terms of both scale and creative expression?

a. Hadrian

b. Nero

c. Julius Caesar

d. Diocletian

306. What is the name of the system of roads built by Rome's first emperor?

a. Appian Way

b. Aurelian Road

c. Trajan's Road

d. Augustus' Path

307. What is considered the main innovation of ancient Roman art compared to that of ancient Greece?

a. Better depiction of Christian motifs

b. Advancement of oil painting techniques

c. Development of techniques like perspective

d. None of the above

ANSWERS

288. d. All of the above
289. a. Tall, slim figures with realistic proportions
290. d. Stone blocks
291. b. Concrete
292. d. Hadrian
293. c. Trajan
294. b. Trajan
295. d. All of the above
296. c. Rome
297. d. All of the above
298. a. Pliny
299. b. Dacian Wars
300. b. Achievements of the Pax Romana
301. b. Aqueducts
302. a. Pons Sublicius
303. c. 80 CE
304. d. Rome
305. a. Hadrian
306. a. Appian Way
307. c. Development of techniques like perspective

Science and Technology

From militarization to trade, the advancement of science and technology has always been fundamental to Rome's prosperity. In this chapter, you'll explore how ancient Roman scientists and engineers created a series of incredible inventions. From new forms of measuring distances to early steam engines, you'll learn all about the advances in science and technology that enabled ancient Rome to build a powerful empire. Challenge your knowledge with a collection of trivia questions that will cover topics like astronomy, mechanics, engineering, and medicine. Engage in some ancient Roman science and technology fun.

308. What was the *cursus publicus*?

a. A public works agency

b. The Senate's first decree on public goods

c. A state-run courier system

d. None of the above

309. Which emperor introduced the *cursus publicus*?

a. Octavian Augustus

b. Nero

c. Maximian

d. Aurelian

310. Which of these was not a use of the aqueducts?

a. Crop irrigation

b. Transportation of water

c. Demarcation of boundaries

d. None of the above

311. What scientific discovery was made by Archimedes, a mathematician from ancient Rome?

a. Laws of motion

b. Atom structure

c. Theory of gravity

d. Principles of buoyancy

312. What technological innovation allowed Romans to build durable structures like the Colosseum and the Pantheon?

a. Fired clay bricks

b. Iron reinforcement

c. Hydraulic cement (Roman concrete)

d. Stone vaulting

313. What form of measurement did the ancient Romans use to calculate distances between locations?

a. Leagues

b. Miles

c. Meters

d. All of the above

314. Which Roman writer documented agricultural science, architecture, and engineering in *De architectura*?

a. Galen

b. Vitruvius

c. Pliny the Elder

d. Seneca

315. What was a hypocaust in ancient Rome?

a. A type of military siege weapon

b. An early system of indoor plumbing

c. An underfloor heating system used in baths and villas

d. A device for pumping water uphill

ANSWERS

308. c. State-run courier system

309. a. Octavian Augustus

310. c. Demarcation of boundaries

311. d. Principles of buoyancy

312. c. Hydraulic cement (Roman concrete)

313. a. Leagues

314. b. Vitruvius

315. c. An underfloor heating system used in baths and villas

Economics and Trade

The Roman Empire is considered one of world history's greatest and most influential empires. For many centuries, Rome not only dominated politics within Europe but also had a great influence on the economy beyond its borders. This chapter will explore some interesting facts related to economics and trade during these times, from the Roman currency to state price control regulations, goods available at marketplaces, trade networks extending through distant lands like India via the Silk Road, and much more.

316. What was the name of the Roman currency?

    a. Dollar

    b. Peso

    c. Lira

    d. Denarius

317. Who officially regulated markets and enforced price controls in ancient Rome?

    a. The Senate

    b. The emperor

    c. Local merchants

    d. State officials

318. Which emperor issued an edict that set maximum prices for important goods in the empire?

a. Diocletian

b. Constantine

c. Trajan

d. Hadrian

319. Which trade route connected India to China via Egypt, Syria, Anatolia, and Mesopotamia?

a. Silk Road

b. Spice Route

c. Mediterranean Sea Trade Route

d. None of the above

320. What was the second largest city in the Roman Empire after Rome before the founding of Constantinople?

a. Jerusalem

b. Ravenna

c. Alexandria

d. Athens

321. What was the most important export of Roman North Africa?

a. Slaves

b. Textiles

c. Agricultural products

d. Pottery

322. Which of these regions supplied the most grain to Rome?

a. Italia

b. Asia Minor

c. Iberia

d. Egypt

323. Which Roman province had rich silver and gold deposits?

a. Germania

b. Iberia

c. Arabia

d. All of the above

324. How did the Romans refer to the Mediterranean Sea?

a. Sea of Peoples

b. Mare Nostrum

c. Euxeinos Pontos

d. None of the above

325. With which ancient civilization did Rome trade luxury items such as silk, glassware, ivory, and spices?

a. Greece

b. Persia

c. Mongolia

d. China

326. Which province produced the most iron for Rome?

a. Italia

b. Hispania

c. North Africa

d. Egypt

327. What was the main commodity of the Roman Empire?

a. Olive oil

b. Metals

c. Spices

d. Grain

328. Which was the richest Roman province in the first century CE?

a. Italy

b. Egypt

c. Asia Minor

d. Iberia

329. What was depicted on ancient Roman coins?

a. Roman sculptures

b. Gods and goddesses from mythology

c. Roman emperors

d. Remus and Romulus

330. What was entirely prohibited by Roman law during antiquity?

    a. Slave trade

    b. Money lending

    c. Oil and timber trade

    d. None of the above

331. Which emperor reformed the Roman bureaucracy and administration to allow for a more efficient collection of taxes?

    a. Diocletian

    b. Nero

    c. Theodosius

    d. Caracalla

332. What were the triremes?

    a. A type of ancient Roman ship

    b. Special military units during the later part of the empire

    c. Emperors' handmaidens

    d. Trade unions

333. What did "fasces" symbolize in Roman culture?

    a. Knowledge

    b. Justice

    c. Wealth

    d. Power

334. Who was the first to establish free grain distributions to citizens from public funds during his reign as emperor?

    a. Julius Caesar

    b. Augustus Caesar

    c. Tiberius

    d. Nero

335. Which of these provinces was the poorest in the Roman Empire?

    a. Syria

    b. Egypt

    c. Germania

    d. Italia

ANSWERS

316. d. Denarius

317. d. State officials

318. a. Diocletian

319. a. Silk Road

320. c. Alexandria

321. c. Agricultural products

322. d. Egypt

323. b. Iberia

324. b. Mare Nostrum

325. d. China

326. b. Hispania

327. d. Grain

328. a. Italy

329. c. Roman emperors

330. d. None of the above

331. a. Diocletian

332. a. A type of ancient Roman ship

333. d. Power

334. b. Augustus Caesar

335. c. Germania

Military Organization and Strategy in Ancient Rome

From Julius Caesar and his legions to the Praetorian Guard of ancient Rome, explore the military organization and strategies of one of history's greatest empires. Learn about recruitment for service in military roles such as the centurion, legate, tribune, or praetor. Examine Roman soldiers' weapons, discover how ancient Romans organized into legions, and uncover where wars occurred during Roman Republic periods—from Italy to Gaul and the Middle East to Britain—while understanding who decided on strategy. Finally, explore topics such as unit sizes for armies, rewards given to distinguished soldiers, types of fortifications, naval warfare, fleets, and which battle formations determined victory over enemies on open fields. You'll find all these answers plus much more when you unlock *Ancient Rome Trivia*: Military Organization and Strategy.

336. What was the highest military rank in ancient Rome?

a. Centurion

b. Legatus

c. Tribune

d. Praetor

337. What was the average number of years a Roman soldier served in the army?

a. Ten years

b. Five years

c. Twenty-five years

d. Unlimited

338. Which emperor fixed the regular term of service for Roman soldiers at sixteen years?

a. Octavian Augustus

b. Julius Caesar

c. Nero

d. None of the above

339. Who were the evocati?

a. Roman archer legions

b. Reservists for the army

c. Elite troops for the emperor

d. None of the above

340. Where did most Roman wars take place during the republic period?

a. Italy

b. Gaul

c. Middle East

d. Britain

341. What was the name of the Roman unit with up to 500 soldiers?

a. Cohort

b. Tribe

c. Company

d. Legion

342. What was the largest unit of a Roman army?

a. Legion

b. Cohort

c. Company

d. Battalion

343. When were the Marian reforms instituted?

    a. 103 CE

    b. 105 CE

    c. 107 CE

    d. 109 CE

344. Who decided on general military strategy in the Roman Empire?

    a. Senate

    b. Praetor

    c. Emperor

    d. Legate

345. What was the standard of the Roman army?

    a. Wolf

    b. Bear

    c. Lion

    d. Eagle

346. When did the Battle of the Teutoburg Forest take place?

    a. 9 CE

    b. 10 CE

    c. 11 CE

    d. 12 CE

347. Who emerged victorious in the Battle of the Teutoburg Forest?

    a. Rome

    b. Germanic tribes

    c. Carthage

    d. Parthia

348. When did the Battle of Adrianople take place?

    a. 371 CE

    b. 380 CE

    c. 378 CE

    d. 374 CE

349. How were soldiers rewarded for distinguished service in ancient Rome?

a. Money

b. Honorary titles

c. Land grants

d. All of the above

350. Which of these troops were non-Roman citizens?

a. Auxiliaries

b. Legionaries

c. Equites

d. Triarii

351. When did the Battle of the Catalaunian Fields take place?

a. Fifth century CE

b. Second century CE

c. First century BCE

d. Third century CE

352. Which was the decisive battle of the Third Samnite Wars?

a. Carrhae

b. Sentinum

c. Zama

d. Pharsalus

353. Up to how many men could each Roman galley hold during naval warfare?

a. 80

b. 100

c. 300

d. 400

354. Which emperor conquered Gaul for Rome?

a. Trajan

b. Hadrian

c. Julius Caesar

d. Octavian Augustus

355. Which famous general defeated Hannibal at the Battle of Zama in 202 BCE to end the Second Punic War?

a. Scipio Africanus

b. Pompey Magnus

c. Marcus Aurelius

d. Claudius

356. How many cavalry were included in the Roman legions during the republic era?

a. 100

b. 200

c. 300

d. 400

357. Who managed to conquer Egypt for Rome?

a. Julius Caesar

b. Mark Antony

c. Augustus

d. Constantine

358. How many men did the standing army number by the end of Augustus' reign?

a. 100,000

b. 250,000

c. 350,000

d. None of the above

359. Who was responsible for the putative reforms of the Roman army in the second century CE?

a. Hadrian

b. Gaius Marius

c. Trajan

d. Polybius

360. What constituted the core of the Roman army?

a. Heavy infantry

b. Light cavalry

c. Archers

d. Pikemen

336. b. Legatus

337. c. Twenty-five years

338. a. Octavian Augustus

339. b. Reservists for the army

340. a. Italy

341. a. Cohort

342. a. Legion

343. c. 107 CE

344. c. Emperor

345. d. Eagle

346. a. 9 CE

347. b. Germanic tribes

348. c. 378 CE

349. d. All of the above

350. a. Auxiliaries

351. a. Fifth century CE

352. b. Sentinum

353. c. 300

354. c. Julius Caesar

355. a. Scipio Africanus

356. c. 300

357. c. Augustus

358. b. 250,000

359. b. Gaius Marius

360. a. Heavy infantry

Political Institutions and Legal Developments

Explore the fascinating world of Roman political institutions and legal developments. Discover what life was like in a once-great empire where every move had to be carefully calculated and obedience to the rule of law was paramount. With questions about how many consuls there were during the early Roman Republic, who had ultimate power over legal matters under Roman law, and what type of court system existed in ancient Rome, this chapter will take you back to discuss some key aspects of Roman history. Find out if your knowledge is up-to-date as you answer trivia spanning important topics ranging from civil and property rights to criminal punishment and enforcers.

361. How many consuls were there during the early Roman Republic?

    a. One

    b. Two

    c. Three

    d. Four

362. Who was the consul during the First Punic War?

    a. Gaius Brutus

    b. Marcus Gervinius

    c. Marcus Atilius Regulus

    d. None of the above

363. What was the purpose of a veto in ancient Rome?

a. To allow one person to pass laws

b. To prevent an official from making decisions

c. To stop a law passed by the Senate

d. To nullify another senator's decision

364. Who had ultimate power over legal matters under Roman law?

a. Magistrates

b. Tribune

c. Senate

d. None of the above

365. How long could an individual serve as head magistrate in ancient Rome?

a. Three months

b. Six months

c. One year

d. Two years

366. Which of these principles did the Romans believe was necessary for justice to be served?

a. Equality

b. Mercy

c. Retribution

d. Punishment

367. Which one was the first Roman office open to the plebeians?

a. Legate

b. Tribune

c. Magistrate

d. Senator

368. Which court dealt with private matters between citizens in ancient Rome?

a. Centumviral court

b. Roman Curia

c. Appellate court

d. None of the above

369. When was intermarriage between plebs and patricians allowed in ancient Rome?

  a. 509 BCE

  b. 445 BCE

  c. 321 BCE

  d. 307 BCE

370. What does "ius" mean when referring to Roman law?

  a. Rights

  b. Custom

  c. Justice

  d. Legislation

371. Which of these was the most important source of law in ancient Rome?

  a. Customary law

  b. Written law

  c. Divine law

  d. Natural law

372. How did Roman citizens participate in making laws, other than indirectly through voting?

  a. By submitting a written opinion

  b. By debating with senators

  c. By deliberations in public assemblies

  d. By having a right to veto

373. Which of these was not part of the content of the Twelve Tables?

  a. Civil rights

  b. Land rights

  c. Execution of judgments

  d. Religious rituals

374. Which form of government replaced the Roman Republic after Julius Caesar's death?

  a. Monarchy

  b. Oligarchy

  c. Democracy

  d. Autocracy

375. What type of court existed during imperial rule to judge cases involving slaves and foreigners?

a. Praetorian court

b. Curiate court

c. Consilium

d. Extraordinary courts

376. Who was responsible for administering civil law in imperial Rome?

a. Censors

b. Senators

c. Praetors

d. Magistrates

377. Which tribune is responsible for introducing a range of legal and civic reforms during his tenure in the second century BCE?

a. Gaius Gracchus

b. Lucius Atillius

c. Lucius Junius Brutus

d. None of the above

378. Which of these was possible as part of the civil legal process in ancient Rome?

a. Trial by combat

b. Arbitration in court

c. Arbitration in front of a religious assembly

d. Coin flip

379. What was the purpose of codification during ancient Roman times?

a. To standardize laws across different regions

b. To simplify legal proceedings

c. To create more efficient courts

d. All of the above

380. What is the meaning of the word *curia*?

a. People's law

b. Gathering of men

c. Wisdom house

d. Policeman

381. Which of these ancient Roman legal principles refers to exact retaliation?

a. Mens rea

b. Lex talionis

c. Actus non facit reum

d. Ex post facto

382. Which form of Roman government reduced the functions of the consuls in favor of new offices of equal rank and prestige?

a. Republic

b. Principate

c. Dominate

d. Oligarchy

383. When did the Principate come to an end?

a. 44 CE

b. 284 CE

c. 476 CE

d. 1453 CE

384. Which office was responsible for the maintenance of public buildings in ancient Rome?

a. Aedile

b. Praetor

c. Quaestor

d. Corrector

385. Who introduced the Centuriate Assembly in ancient Rome?

a. Julius Caesar

b. Tarquinius Superbus

c. Servius Tullius

d. Octavian Augustus

ANSWERS

361. b. Two

362. c. Marcus Atilius Regulus

363. b. To prevent an official from making decisions

364. a. Magistrates

365. c. One year

366. c. Retribution

367. b. Tribune

368. a. Centumviral court

369. b. 445 BCE

370. a. Rights

371. b. Written law

372. c. By deliberations in public assemblies

373. d. Religious rituals

374. d. Autocracy

375. d. Extraordinary courts

376. c. Praetors

377. a. Gaius Gracchus

378. b. Arbitration in court

379. d. All of the above

380. b. Gathering of men

381. b. Lex talionis

382. b. Principate

383. b. 284 CE

384. a. Aedile

385. c. Servius Tullius

Slavery and Social Class Hierarchy

The ancient Roman Empire was a complex social order, and slavery took on many forms in the Roman world. For example, those without full political rights could be reduced to working without freedom or autonomy. This chapter of *Ancient Rome Trivia* will explore the various aspects of slavery, from how it came to exist during this period to how people obtained their freedom and finally assumed their social class within society. Learn what the term *servus* meant, when slavery saw its peak, and what types of punishments were put in place for disobedient slaves. Test your knowledge even further with some intriguing trivia questions.

386. What was the common Latin word for "slave" in ancient Rome?

a. Servus

b. Slavus

c. Centus

d. Cranchus

387. Which was the first Roman emperor to be captured during warfare?

a. Domitian

b. Valerian

c. Vespasian

d. Maximian

388. How could slaves gain their freedom under the Roman Empire?

a. They couldn't become free

b. By becoming athletes and winning competitions

c. Through military service

d. By being granted emancipation by their owners

389. Which class held the highest status within society during ancient Rome?

a. Patricians

b. Plebeians

c. Freedmen

d. Slaves

390. How did wealthy Romans acquire their slaves in ancient Rome?

a. They bought them from foreign traders

b. They inherited them from family members

c. They captured prisoners during war

d. All of the above

391. Under which government was the class division in ancient Rome the clearest?

a. Monarchy to early Roman Republic

b. Late Roman Republic

c. Principate

d. Dominate

392. Who was the legendary slave-born king of ancient Rome?

a. Servius Tullius

b. Tarquinius Superbus

c. Numa Pompilius

d. Ancus Marcius

393. What was the term used to describe a freedman in ancient Rome?

a. Libertus

b. Patronus

c. Burgundus

d. None of the above

394. What is referred to as the Conflict of the Orders?

  a. A civil war during the late Roman Republic

  b. A period of anarchy after the establishment of the Roman Empire

  c. A period of political struggle between the patricians and the plebeians

  d. None of the above

395. What year marks the end of the Conflict of the Orders?

  a. 389 BCE

  b. 287 BCE

  c. 123 CE

  d. 509 BCE

396. Which famous Roman statesman claimed that "law is the highest reason, rooted in nature, which commands things that must be done and prohibits the opposite"?

  a. Pliny

  b. Tacitus

  c. Cato the Elder

  d. Cicero

397. When did the slave rebellions end in the Roman Republic?

  a. 267 BCE

  b. 71 BCE

  c. 59 BCE

  d. 110 BCE

398. The demand for slaves was one of the primary justifications behind the conquest of which of these provinces?

  a. Iberia

  b. Gaul

  c. Britain

  d. Asia Minor

399. Who was the leader of the most famous slave rebellion in ancient Rome?

  a. Constantius

  b. Spartacus

  c. Maximus

  d. Decius

400. How did Roman law define a slave's legal status?

a. Property

b. Person

c. Citizen

d. Freedman

401. Who could legally own slaves during ancient Rome?

a. Senators

b. Patricians

c. Generals

d. All of the above

402. Which form of punishment was most commonly used against disobedient or rebellious slaves in ancient Rome?

a. Whipping

b. Executions

c. Imprisonment

d. None of the above

403. Which of these cities in the Roman Empire had large slave markets?

a. Constantinople

b. Alexandria

c. Capua

d. Rhodos

404. What was the name of the free tenant farmers who appeared in ancient Rome increasingly during the fourth century CE?

a. Coloni

b. Curiatii

c. Decurions

d. Servii

405. About which percentage of the population of the city of Rome consisted of slaves in the first century CE?

a. 10 percent

b. 80 percent

c. 30 percent

d. 45 percent

ANSWERS

386. a. Servus

387. b. Valerian

388. d. By being granted emancipation by their owners

389. a. Patricians

390. d. All of the above

391. a. Monarchy to early Roman Republic

392. a. Servius Tullius

393. a. Libertus

394. c. A period of political struggle between the patricians and the plebeians

395. b. 287 BCE

396. d. Cicero

397. b. 71 BCE

398. c. Britain

399. b. Spartacus

400. a. Property

401. d. All of the above

402. a. Whipping

403. c. Capua

404. a. Coloni

405. c. 30 percent

Agricultural Practices

In ancient Rome, farming was essential for both economic development and food production. The agricultural practices that have gone unchanged since Roman times were determined largely by the climate and soil of the region. Each season brings a new crop to harvest, so it's understandable why the Romans would develop such deep respect for this occupation as well as methods to improve its productivity. In this *Ancient Rome Trivia* chapter, we'll discuss some of the strategies employed by ancient Roman farmers to sustain life during this time—from tilling techniques to harvesting tools. We'll provide you with questions about what type of soil was best suited for certain crops in ancient Rome, how the Romans practiced crop rotation, and which farm animals they kept. Let's dig in together and find out!

406. What type of soil was best suited for growing grapes in ancient Rome?

a. Sandy loam

b. Clay loam

c. Rocky soil

d. Potting mix

407. How did the Romans practice crop rotation?

a. By changing fields each year and alternating between wheat and barley

b. By planting different crops within one field every season

c. By planting multiple plants together to increase water retention

d. By switching between multigrain farming and monoculture farming

408. Which of these tools were used to plow Roman land?

a. Scythe

b. Pickaxe

c. Hoe

d. Ox-drawn plow

409. What method did the ancient Romans use to fertilize their soil with nitrogen?

a. Manure

b. Compost

c. Pesticides

d. Nitrogen fixation

410. Which crop was considered the most important in ancient Rome?

a. Wheat

b. Olives

c. Fruit

d. Barley

411. What did Roman farmers use to measure their fields?

a. Rulers

b. Maps

c. Sticks

d. Measuring wheels

412. Which of these crops were commonly grown by Roman farmers?

a. Millet

b. Rye

c. Sugar beets

d. Tobacco

413. Who was responsible for planting, cultivating, harvesting, and selling farm produce in ancient Rome?

a. Patricians

b. Plebeians

c. Slaves

d. Senate

414. What type of irrigation system was used by ancient Roman farmers?

a. Hydroponics

b. Well-based irrigation

c. Flood-based irrigation

d. Sprinkler system

415. What did the Romans use to store their grain and other produce?

a. Pantries

b. Refrigerators

c. Grain silos

d. Barns

416. What common method did the ancient Romans use to control weeds and pests on their land?

a. Herbicides

b. Watering

c. Mulching

d. Tilling

417. How often did Roman farmers rotate their crops?

a. Every season

b. Every two years

c. Never

d. Annually

418. Which of these is an example of an animal that was kept for agricultural purposes in ancient Rome?

a. Mules

b. Horses

c. Sheep

d. Camels

419. What type of animal was used to pull Roman plows?

a. Cattle

b. Goats

c. Oxen

d. Donkeys

420. What type of tools did Roman farmers use to harvest their crops?

a. Scythes and sickles

b. Hoes and rakes

c. Shovels and forks

d. Axes and hammers

ANSWERS

406. a. Sandy loam

407. b. By planting different crops within one field every season

408. d. Ox-drawn plow

409. a. Manure

410. a. Wheat

411. c. Sticks

412. a. Millet

413. c. Slaves

414. b. Well-based irrigation

415. c. Grain silos

416. d. Tilling

417. b. Every two years

418. a. Mules

419. c. Oxen

420. a. Scythes and sickles

Daily Life

From the day-to-day ordinary to the extraordinary, ancient Rome was full of surprises. In this chapter, we'll explore some fun facts about daily life in ancient Rome. Ever wonder how often Roman citizens visited public baths or what type of clothing they wore? Learn all that and more as you explore daily life in ancient Roman times.

421. How often did the average Roman citizen visit the public baths in ancient Rome?

a. Once per week

b. Twice per day

c. Several times a week

d. A few times each month

422. What was the main meal of the day for most Romans?

a. Ientaculum (breakfast)

b. Cena (dinner)

c. Prandium (lunch)

d. Gustatio (appetizer)

423. What was the most common form of transportation during ancient Roman times?

a. Horses

b. Boats

c. Walking

d. Donkeys

424. Which type of food made up the majority of an average Roman diet?

a. Grains/cereals

b. Meat

c. Vegetables

d. Fruit

425. What type of tool was used by the Romans for writing on papyrus or wax tablets?

a. Pencils

b. Stylus

c. Quill pens

d. Charcoal

426. What type of clothing did Roman citizens wear?

a. Pants

b. Tunics

c. Cloaks

d. Dresses

427. Where did many poor Romans live in the city of Rome?

a. Villas

b. Palaces

c. Insulae (apartment buildings)

d. Domus

428. Which groups were responsible for paying taxes in ancient Rome?

a. The poor

b. The rich

c. Everyone

d. Only the slaves

429. How old were average Roman citizens when they got married?

a. Thirteen to fifteen years old

b. Sixteen to eighteen years old

c. Nineteen to twenty-one years old

d. Twenty-two years or older

430. What were the two main languages spoken in ancient Rome?

a. Latin and Greek

b. Italian and French

c. Spanish and Portuguese

d. German and English

431. How was Roman law divided?

a. Into twelve parts

b. Into three parts

c. By region

d. Into four levels

432. Who had the right to vote in ancient Rome?

a. Freeborn men

b. Slaves

c. Women

d. Everyone

433. Which of these sports was popular among ancient Romans?

a. Football

b. Ice hockey

c. Swimming

d. Gladiatorial combat

434. Where did most marriages take place during ancient Roman times?

a. At home

b. In temples

c. In the Forum

d. At a public gathering

435. What was one popular form of entertainment that took place in ancient Rome?

a. Theatre

b. Wrestling

c. Bull-fighting

d. Concerts

436. How did most Roman citizens get their news?

a. By watching plays

b. From the Senate

c. Through word of mouth

d. Through newspapers

437. What were slaves in ancient Rome usually given as payment for work?

a. Money

b. Food

c. Time off

d. Freedom

438. On what day of the week would Romans not do any work?

a. Monday

b. Saturday

c. They did not have a day off

d. Thursday

439. Who served as magistrates and judges in ancient Rome?

a. Priests

b. Senators

c. Emperors

d. Lawyers

440. What would Roman citizens do to show respect for their emperor?

a. Bow

b. Salute

c. Cheer

d. All of the above

421. c. Several times a week

422. b. Cena (dinner)

423. c. Walking

424. a. Grains/cereals

425. b. Stylus

426. b. Tunics

427. c. Insulae (apartment buildings)

428. c. Everyone

429. b. Sixteen to eighteen years old

430. a. Latin and Greek

431. b. Into three parts

432. a. Freeborn men

433. d. Gladiatorial combat

434. a. At home

435. a. Theatre

436. c. Through word of mouth

437. b. Food

438. c. They do not have a day off

439. b. Senators

440. d. All of the above

Foreign Relations of Ancient Rome with Carthage, Greece, and Other Nations

Throughout history, ancient Rome was one of the most powerful and influential empires in the world. Its foreign policy included complex networks of alliances with conquered peoples and other nations to maintain control over their territories and colonies. In this chapter, we'll explore how these relationships forged by the Romans shaped politics for centuries to come. From establishing military outposts to negotiating trade treaties or waging war against rival empires, Roman leaders used many tactics to dominate their neighbors politically. We'll learn about Julius Caesar's role in negotiating peace treaties with various entities across Europe and his campaigns against enemy forces who fought fiercely to protect their independence. Finally, we'll examine Rome's use of economic sanctions and other diplomatic strategies to benefit from trade agreements or influence allies and enemies alike.

441. What did Rome do to ensure it had control over its territories and colonies during its empire?

a. Established military outposts throughout the region

b. Set up administrative entities to rule in the name of Rome

c. Built extensive roads connecting regions

d. All of the above

---

442. With which Egyptian ruler did Julius Caesar negotiate?

a. King Ramses II

b. Queen Cleopatra VII

c. King Tut

d. King Ahmose

443. Which Roman emperor led major campaigns against the Sassanid Empire?

a. Augustus

b. Trajan

c. Constantine

d. Septimus Severus

444. When did the Roman-Seleucid Wars begin?

a. 199 CE

b. 199 BCE

c. 192 CE

d. 192 BCE

445. When was Corinth destroyed by the Romans?

a. 153 BCE

b. 150 BCE

c. 146 BCE

d. 140 BCE

446. When did the First Mithridatic War take place?

a. 100-105 CE

b. 89-85 BCE

c. 78-70 BCE

d. 39-48 CE

447. How did Julius Caesar play an important role in Rome's foreign relations?

a. He negotiated a peace treaty with Persia

b. He conducted negotiations for a trade agreement with India

c. He led a successful offensive against the Germanic barbarians

d. He legally established a protectorate over Egypt

448. Which treaty marked the end of the First Mithridatic War?

    a. Treaty of Dardanos

    b. Treaty of Pontus

    c. Treaty of Bithynia

    d. Treaty of Corinth

449. Who were the foederati?

    a. Members of the government during the Principate

    b. Local federalist rebels under Octavian

    c. Mercenary barbarians that fought for Rome

    d. Military commanders of the First Mithridatic War

450. Why was Julius Caesar's planned invasion of the Parthian Empire aborted?

    a. Parthia collapsed before he could invade

    b. There was a civil war he had to deal with

    c. He was assassinated

    d. He negotiated a peace agreement with Parthia

451. What did ancient Greece gain from its alliance with Rome during the Punic Wars?

    a. Military protection against barbarians

    b. Economic support for its colonies

    c. Access to Roman knowledge and technology

    d. All of the above

452. Who was the leader of the Roman army during the Battle of Vellica?

    a. Julius Caesar

    b. Octavian Augustus

    c. Nero

    d. Trajan

453. Which Roman emperor fought in the battles of Issus, Lugdunum, and Ctesiphon?

    a. Hadrian

    b. Marcus Aurelius

    c. Septimus Severus

    d. Maximian

454. When was the First Peace of Nisibis negotiated?

   a. 299 CE

   b. 311 CE

   c. 321 CE

   d. 329 CE

455. What was the main purpose of Julius Caesar's diplomatic mission to Egypt in 48 BCE?

   a. To convince Cleopatra to marry him

   b. To punish Mark Antony for fleeing to Egypt

   c. To mediate a succession dispute between Cleopatra and Ptolemy XIII

   d. All of the above

456. Who emerged victorious from the Achaean War?

   a. Achaean League

   b. Rome

   c. Peloponnesian city-states

   d. Neither side

457. When was the Latin League formed?

   a. 200 BCE

   b. 300 BCE

   c. 400 BCE

   d. 500 BCE

458. Who was the Macedonian king during the First Macedonian War?

   a. Alexander

   b. Philip II

   c. Philip V

   d. Antigonus

459. Who defeated Emperor Theodosius I in 380 in the Battle of Thessalonica?

   a. Galatians

   b. Goths

   c. Huns

   d. Sassanids

460. Who did the Romans defeat at the Siege of Massilia in 413 CE?

a. Visigoths

b. Ostrogoths

c. Huns

d. Vandals

ANSWERS

441. d. All of the above

442. b. Queen Cleopatra VII

443. d. Septimus Severus

444. d. 192 BCE

445. c. 146 BCE

446. b. 89-85 BCE

447. c. He led a successful offensive against the Germanic barbarians

448. a. Treaty of Dardanos

449. c. Mercenary barbarians that fought for Rome

450. c. He was assassinated

451. b. Economic support for their colonies

452. b. Octavian Augustus

453. c. Septimus Severus

454. a. 299 CE

455. c. To mediate a succession dispute between Cleopatra VII and Ptolemy XIII

456. b. Rome

457. d. 500 BCE

458. c. Philip V

459. b. Goths

460. a. Visigoths

Development of the Latin Language

Latin has long been considered one of the most influential languages in history. Since it emerged as the language of ancient Rome, it has shaped cultures and societies around the globe. In this chapter, we will explore some trivia about Latin's development in ancient Rome—from what language it evolved from to how members of different social classes used Latin differently over time. We'll also examine questions such as when writing was adopted from Rome's neighbors, what significant event sparked changes in its evolution, which other languages influenced Roman literature, and how Latin spread during its height. So, dive deep with us now for a stimulating journey through ancient wonders!

461. What was the language spoken in Rome before Latin?

   a. Greek

   b. Etruscan

   c. Sumerian

   d. Egyptian

462. When did the Romans adopt writing from their Etruscan neighbors?

   a. Sixth century BCE

   b. Second century BCE

   c. Seventh century BCE

   d. Fourth century CE

463. How was Latin used by the common people of Rome during its height?

a. As a formal, written language only

b. As an informal, spoken dialect only

c. Both formally and informally

d. Neither formally nor informally

464. Which major event is thought to have sparked significant changes in the development of the Latin language in ancient Rome?

a. The Punic Wars

b. Julius Caesar's rise to power

c. The fall of Hannibal

d. The Great Fire

465. Who wrote *De lingua Latina*, one of the earliest surviving works on Latin grammar?

a. Julius Caesar

b. Cicero

c. Virgil

d. Varro

466. What is a major difference between Classical and Vulgar Latin?

a. The first was more for the elite and literary purposes, while the second was more for common use

b. The first was mainly for religious purposes, while the second included secular contexts

c. The first used more complex syntax than the second

d. The first used more consonants than the second

467. Literary works in what language heavily influenced early Roman literature?

a. Spanish

b. Greek

c. German

d. Etruscan

468. What was the art of public speaking called in ancient Rome?

a. Drama

b. Oratoria

c. Comoedia

d. Liturgia

469. Which century marked the end of Classical Latin and the beginning of Late Latin as the literary standard in ancient Rome?

a. First century CE

b. Second century CE

c. Third century CE

d. Fourth century CE

470. What was the lingua franca of the territories of the Eastern Roman Empire?

a. Aramaic

b. Latin

c. Phoenician

d. Greek

471. What helped the spread of the Latin language in Europe in the late Roman Empire?

a. Its adoption by migrating Germanic peoples

b. Laws enacted by Emperor Theodosius

c. The collapse of the Western Roman Empire

d. All of the above

472. Which of these is not a literary form of Latin recognized by scholars?

a. Classical Latin

b. Vulgar Latin

c. Medieval Latin

d. Old Latin

473. Which of these is responsible for preserving and developing the Latin language after the fall of the Western Roman Empire?

a. The Catholic Church

b. Eastern Roman Empire

c. Imperial College of the Holy Roman Empire

d. Knights Templar

474. Which of these ancient Roman writers did Petrarch regard as "the third great light of Rome"?

a. Virgil

b. Cicero

c. Varro

d. Tacitus

475. Who wrote *De rerum natura* (*On the Nature of Things*), one of the earliest surviving works written in Classical Latin?

a. Cicero

b. Virgil

c. Lucretius

d. Varro

476. Which of these ancient writers wrote *De Re Publica* (*On the Republic*)?

a. Cicero

b. Lucretius

c. Varro

d. Pliny

477. How did the Roman Empire use Latin to unify its culture?

a. As an official language in court proceedings

b. By creating standardized laws and regulations

c. By establishing educational standards

d. All of the above

478. What was one major factor that contributed to the decline of Classical Latin in Rome?

a. The influence of Greek literature

b. Rapid population growth

c. A shift away from traditional values

d. Growing popularity of Christianity

479. Who wrote *De Bello Gallico*, which details Julius Caesar's campaigns during his conquest of Gaul?

a. Cicero

b. Virgil

c. Livy

d. Julius Caesar

480. The work of which of these authors is considered to be a seminal piece about the Second Punic War?

a. Cicero

c. Livy

b. Pliny

d. Scipio

ANSWERS

461. b. Etruscan

462. c. seventh century BCE

463. c. Both formally and informally

464. b. Julius Caesar's rise to power

465. d. Varro

466. a. The former was more for the elite and literary practices, while the latter was more for common use

467. b. Greek

468. b. Oratoria

469. c. Third century CE

470. d. Greek

471. a. Its adoption by migrating Germanic peoples

472. b. Vulgar Latin

473. a. The Catholic Church

474. c. Varro

475. c. Lucretius

476. a. Cicero

477. d. All of the above

478. d. Growing popularity of Christianity

479. d. Caesar

480. c. Livy

Legacy of Ancient Rome

The legacy of ancient Rome extends far beyond the demise of its powerful empire and long-lasting cultural influence. The origins and development of this majestic civilization are revealed in snippets found throughout history, leading to a highly complex tale that is still being unraveled today. This chapter focuses on the fascinating legacy of ancient Rome. Put your knowledge of Roman culture to the test with these twenty questions about some of its most prominent features. Challenge yourself with each question as you explore this unprecedented period through trivia.

481. What was the Latin phrase used to refer to the Roman Empire?

a. Imperium Romanum

b. Urbs Aeterna

c. Pax Romana

d. Roma Invicta

482. How long did Rome's legal system remain in use after its fall?

a. Several centuries

b. Several decades

c. Two centuries

d. One century

483. What do we call the period of cultural, economic, and political recovery during which Europe re-established itself as a major center of power after the fall of Rome?

a. The Renaissance

b. The Reformation

c. The Enlightenment

d. The Industrial Revolution

484. Which European country adopted Christianity as its official religion following Emperor Constantine's conversion in 312 CE?

a. France

b. Spain

c. Italy

d. Greece

485. What was the name of Julius Caesar's adopted son who became Emperor Augustus?

a. Nero

b. Tiberius

c. Caligula

d. Octavian

486. How did Roman civilization influence art, architecture, and engineering in Europe?

a. By introducing Christianity

b. By developing new methods of warfare

c. By creating aqueducts and roads

d. By reviving Greco-Roman traditions

487. Which Roman emperor is famous for having built a wall to protect Britain from northern invasions?

a. Marcus Aurelius

b. Trajan

c. Constantine

d. Hadrian

488. What are the two main languages that evolved from Latin, the language spoken in ancient Rome?

a. Spanish and French

b. German and Italian

c. English and Portuguese

d. Dutch and Danish

489. Who was levied to fill the ranks of Rome's legions?

a. Slaves

b. Women

c. Roman citizens

d. Mercenary soldiers

490. What was the name of the large estates on which wealthy Romans lived and farmed?

a. Villas

b. Latifundia

c. Domus

d. Insulae

491. What term is used to describe an administrative region under Roman rule?

a. Province

b. Municipium

c. Colony

d. Kingdom

492. What was the name of Rome's powerful Senate?

a. Consilium

b. Comitia

c. Curia

d. Collegium

493. What is the Latin term for Roman law?

a. Ius civile

b. Lex Romana

c. Corpus iuris civilis

d. Jus gentium

494. How did ancient Romans use aqueducts to transport water across long distances?

a. By using wheels and pulleys

b. By using slaves

c. By building canals

d. By constructing bridges

495. What is the Latin term for Roman roads?

a. Via Romana

b. Strata

c. Calcis Via

d. Via Appia

496. Which Roman politician wrote a philosophical treatise called *De Officiis*?

a. Julius Caesar

b. Cicero

c. Augustus

d. Marcus Aurelius

497. How did ancient Rome influence modern democracy in Europe and the United States?

a. By introducing Christianity

b. By inspiring revolutions

c. By establishing representative government

d. By creating aqueducts and roads

498. How long was it before Italy was unified following the fall of Rome in 476 CE?

a. Five centuries

b. Two centuries

c. Fourteen centuries

d. Ten centuries

499. What were the two main routes used by Roman traders to transport goods from one part of the empire to another?

a. The Silk Road and the Sahara desert routes

b. The Mediterranean Sea and Adriatic Sea

c. The Danube River and Rhine River

d. The Nile River and Euphrates River

500. What is an example of a legacy left behind by ancient Rome that still exists today?

a. Currency

b. Aqueducts

c. Roads

d. Language

ANSWERS

481. a. Imperium Romanum

482. b. Several centuries

483. a. The Renaissance

484. b. Italy

485. d. Octavian

486. c. By creating aqueducts and roads

487. d. Hadrian

488. a. Spanish and French

489. c. Roman citizens

490. a. Latifundia

491. a. Province

492. b. Comitia

493. a. Ius civile

494. d. By constructing bridges

495. a. Via Romana

496. b. Cicero

497. c. By establishing representative government

498. b. Fourteen centuries

499. b. The Mediterranean Sea and Adriatic Sea

500. b. Aqueducts

Conclusion

Throughout this book, we have explored the various facets of ancient Rome and its lasting legacy. We began by learning about the founding of the city-state in 753 BCE and its rise to become one of history's largest empires.

As it expanded, Roman culture developed through art, literature, music, science, and technology, as well as political institutions such as law and government structures, which still influence many aspects of modern life today.

The Punic Wars with Carthage were a defining moment for Rome that set it on its path toward global domination for centuries. Julius Caesar's military conquests laid the groundwork for Augustus' Pax Romana period. His death ushered in an era of civil war between several dynasties until Constantine I declared Christianity as Rome's official religion during his reign from 306 CE to 337 CE.

Finally, we examined how foreign relations shaped ancient Rome's relationship with other nations like Greece or Carthage. We also looked at agricultural practices that sustained daily life until Rome's eventual fall in 476 CE. Despite its fall, Rome's impact on our modern world remains as strong today as it ever was, and its legacy will continue to live on for many generations to come.

Check out another book in the series

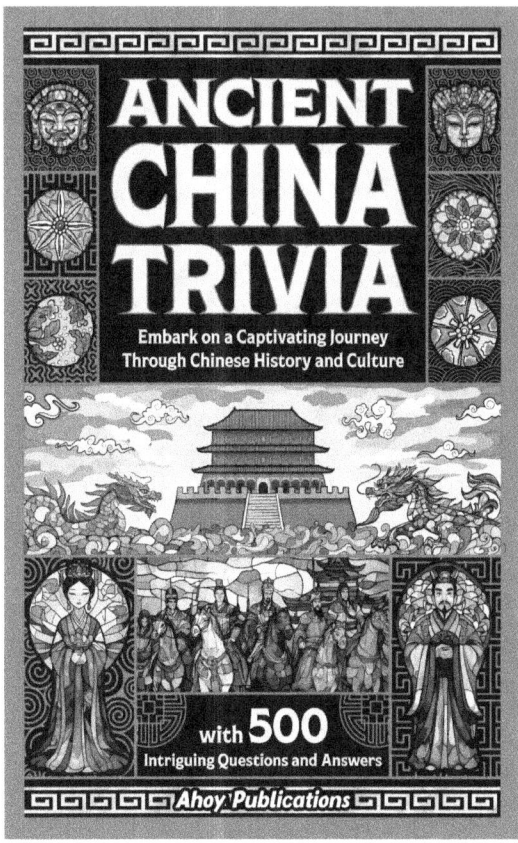

Welcome Aboard, Check Out This Limited-Time Free Bonus!

Ahoy, reader! Welcome to the Ahoy Publications family, and thanks for snagging a copy of this book! Since you've chosen to join us on this journey, we'd like to offer you something special.

Check out the link below for a FREE e-book filled with delightful facts about American History.

But that's not all - you'll also have access to our exclusive email list with even more free e-books and insider knowledge. Well, what are ye waiting for? Click the link below to join and set sail toward exciting adventures in American History.

Access your bonus here

https://ahoypublications.com/

Or, Scan the QR code!